Working Alone

The Institute of Management (IM) is at the forefront of management development and best management practice. The Institute embraces all levels of management from students to chief executives. It provides a unique portfolio of services for all managers, enabling them to develop skills and achieve management excellence. If you would like to hear more about the benefits of mem-bership, please write to Department P, Institute of Management, Cottingham Road, Corby NN17 1TT. This series is commissioned by the Institute of Management Foundation.

The Suzy Lamplugh Trust is the National Charity for Personal Safety. The Trust's work is preventative: a positive reaction to aggression and violence which in its many forms seems endemic in society today. Through research, education and training, the Trust, in seeking a safer society, enables people to go about their daily lives with increased confidence and without fear, living life to the full.

All royalties earned by Diana Lamplugh from this book are donated to The Suzy Lamplugh Trust.

Working Alone

Surviving and Thriving

■

MIKE WOODS
and
JACKIE WHITEHEAD

in association with
DIANA LAMPLUGH, OBE

in the Institute
of Management
PITMAN PUBLISHING

Our book is written for the men and women who, as part of their duties, work without the immediate support of colleagues and often away from their home base – Lone Workers.

The book is intended to be positive in its approach, accepting that many Lone Workers enjoy working alone.

Its aim is that such work can be done at less risk.

Its audience is both the Lone Workers themselves and their managers.

Pitman Publishing
128 Long Acre, London WC2E 9AN

A Division of Longman Group UK Limited

First published in 1993

© Diana Lamplugh, Michael Woods and
Jacqueline Whitehead 1993

A CIP catalogue record for this book can be obtained
from the British Library.

ISBN 0 273 60196 2

All rights reserved; no part of this publication may be
reproduced, stored in a retrieval system, or transmitted in
any form or by any means, electronic, mechanical, photocopying,
recording, or otherwise without either the prior written permission
of the Publishers or a licence permitting restricted copying issued
by the Copyright Licensing Agency, 90 Tottenham Court Road,
London W1P 9HE. This book may not be lent, resold, hired out or
otherwise disposed of by way of trade in any form of binding
or cover other than that in which it is published,
without the prior consent of the Publishers

Typeset by PanTek Arts, Maidstone, Kent.
Printed and bound in Great Britain
by Bell and Bain Ltd, Glasgow

Contents

∎

Foreword by Diana Lamplugh	ix
Acknowledgements	xii
Introduction	xiii

1 WHAT DOES BEING A LONE WORKER MEAN? 1
  Introducing Alan and Barbara 1
  The job, the environment and the job holder 6
  Meeting individual psychological needs 10

2 THE ENJOYMENT OF WORKING ALONE 17
  The 'bears and squares' 17
  The Lone Worker and self-motivation 20
  Stress and the Lone Worker 23
  Stress and the balance of 'people needs' 27
  Support mechanisms 33

3 BETTER SAFE THAN SORRY – PLANNING TO AVOID HAZARDS 35
  Legal responsibilities for safe working 36
  Establishing safe working procedures 39
  Diagnosis: identifying potential risks 41
  Prognosis: collation and classification of incident data 44
  Treatment: action to reduce risks 48
  Health care 49
  Guidelines for safe working 49

4 NOBODY WANTS DEAD HEROES 58
  Eileen and the angry farmer 58
  Agreeing on objectives 60
  Different roles need different tactics 63
  Setting objectives 65
  Personal maintenance 67

5 POINTS OF RISK — 69
- What is aggression? — 69
- Hazardous things, hazardous people — 73
- The principle of the 'traffic lights' — 76

6 BEHAVING YOURSELF INTO TROUBLE — 81
- The messages, messengers and shadows — 81
- Preconceptions — 84
- Physical characteristics — 85
- Dress — 85
- The words and the language we use — 86
- Non-verbal behaviour — 88
- The total communication package — 90
- Showing empathy — 93
- Planning for effective communication — 97

7 I CAN HEAR WHAT YOU SAY BUT I CAN SEE WHAT YOU MEAN — 104
- Attitude problems — 105
- The Attitude Loop — 107
- Stopping the Attitude Loop – use the STOP sign — 109
- Reviewing negative internal dialogue — 110
- Classifying negative internal dialogue — 112
- Resisting pressure — 117
- Dealing with criticism — 119
- Giving criticism — 124
- Professional distancing — 125

8 STRESS AND ANXIETY IN A CONFLICT SITUATION — 127
- Debbie and the cup of coffee too far — 127
- What makes events stressful? — 128
- Why it is important to know how we react to potential danger — 133
- Perception and the appraisal of 'threat' — 134
- How to handle anxiety — 137
- Coming to terms with a traumatic experience — 140
- Counselling for victims of incidents — 144

**9 THE GREAT DEBATE – DRAWING THE LINE
SOMEWHERE** **148**
Should we be trained in self-defence techniques? 148
Equality? 150

Appendix 1: An example of a violent incident report form *153*

Appendix 2: Safety guidelines for Lone Workers *156*

Appendix 3: Stress counselling *163*

Appendix 4: Assessing stress and the Lone Worker *170*

*Appendix 5: The Health and Safety regulations
       in force from January 1993* *172*

Appendix 6: Safety awareness programme for Lone Workers *176*

Appendix 7: Useful addresses *178*

Bibliography *180*

Index *182*

Foreword

■

'This', I thought after my first meeting with these two enthusiastic people, 'is an important piece of the jigsaw; a vital addition in the Trust's quest to enable people to live safer lives.'

When I first read the manuscript for *Working Alone* several months later I realised that my first instincts had been correct. This book, written by those two authors, should become an essential read for everyone who works on their own, through choice or necessity.

Mike Woods and Jackie Whitehead have produced a book which is quite excellent. It is most informative, useful and almost compulsive reading for an addict like myself. Indeed I became quite 'hooked' and am sure I will return to sections again and again.

I also became quite concerned that maybe I understood the material too well as I was overfamiliar with the subject, so I asked two young people who were not so committed and informed for their judgement. They reported that they found it fascinating and revealing.

I wondered how they would survive the tests, the games, the hard work. Like all good training material, this book forces reader participation and application. 'It's good', they said, 'it makes us think.' 'Do you know, it says here . . .' and they were away, proudly teaching their grandmother to suck eggs. They, too, could not let it go.

Since my daughter disappeared while going about her normal daily work as an Estate Agent Negotiator, it has become abundantly clear that violence at work is a very real problem. All the indicators point to an unprecedented rise in violent and aggressive incidents and attacks which take place either in the workplace or in the course of our work, and the number of reported incidents is rising all the time.

Violence at work is not just physical. Employees face verbal and mental abuse, discrimination, harassment, bullying and even ostracism,

Anyone can be the victim of such an attack. It is not just those in high profile jobs such as the police. Staff in a whole range of public and private sector organisations – from the social services to teaching, from the leisure industry to financial retailing – can and do face violence and aggression at work. In fact the greater your contact with the general public the greater the risk. Nor is it just women who are affected; men are actually more at risk than women.

It would seem wise for the management to take the appropriate steps:

- to develop and implement policies to protect their staff and helpers from violence at work (in all its forms);
- to give training to help the workers to deal with problems associated with violence and aggression constructively;
- to enable staff to understand and lessen the risks, avoid or defuse dangerous situations, and only as a last resort, take actions to deal with any violent attack.

The Suzy Lamplugh Trust has produced a very helpful manual which provides detailed guidelines for the nontrainer on planning, designing and delivering personal safety training plus suggested programme outlines for training different levels of staff.

However this is the first time we have been involved with an attempt to provide guidance for those who often need help most – those who work alone – just as Suzy did so many years ago now.

The HSE and EEC regulations state that once the employer has undertaken Personal Safety Risk Assessment for their employees and met this with training, procedures and action then the employees' responsibility is not to put themselves, their colleagues or workplace in danger.

This book should help everyone. Knowledge gives you freedom – to choose, to make informed decisions, to act upon them and to work well and without anxiety.

This book is being published just seven years since Suzy disappeared. She is now presumed murdered and it is at seven years that Suzy will legally be declared dead.

Suzy was a Lone Worker, this book would have helped her – it will undoubtedly help many others to live without fear and be able to work well and safely. We see this work as part of her legacy.

Diana Lamplugh OBE
29 April 1993

Acknowledgements

The authors would like to thank the following people for their help and advice:

Cathryn Leach and Peter Deacon of the National Rivers Authority for the original concept; John Stone for the legal advice; Len Davies of the Yorkshire Water Authority for assistance with the chapters on stress; Jenny Finder of Bradford Management Centre for the information searches.

Introduction

■

A major problem of today's society is the increasing number of violent attacks against ordinary people carrying out their normal work. The attacks can happen to virtually anyone and are certainly not confined to any specific group in society – women, the police or military personnel. There is, however, a *classification* of worker particularly at risk – the Lone Worker. For the Lone Worker not only the risk, but also the consequences of attack are greater – the worker among colleagues has both their protection and their immediate care should an attack occur.

Lone Workers can be defined as those working in situations where they are the sole representative of their calling or organisation.

The classification of Lone Workers cuts across a myriad of jobs and professions linked only by the fact that it involves work which, at least some of the time, has to be done without the continuous support of colleagues. Among our list of Lone Worker occupations and callings we will find social workers, nurses, journalists, postal delivery workers, many teachers and trainers, taxi drivers, bar staff, salespeople, collectors and inspectors, many policemen and women, receptionists, general practitioners, referees and umpires . . . the list is long.

The Lone Worker may be working inside or outside and the actual place of work may be remote or public. For our purposes someone striding across a moorland, working in a laboratory, delivering letters in a crowded housing estate or stuck on a motorway can all classify as Lone Workers. If they are working without the immediate support and assistance of colleagues then they are Lone Workers.

If it can be so dangerous to work alone, why is Lone Working legal in the first place? Some lone working is not legal; working with live electrical equipment or in confined spaces, working with high speed machinery or rowing a boat are specific examples. However, outside these and other specific examples, provided reasonable care is taken, lone working is perfectly legal. Also, as we will see in the first chapters, it is a preferred way of working for many people.

In talking to many Lone Workers, we are struck by several things:

- Firstly, not all those who we would classify as Lone Workers would accept the label. It may be difficult to accept that teachers working with dozens of students or children are Lone Workers but, by our definition, they are. Teachers are, for a considerable part of their working lives, the sole representatives of their calling among children or students whose concerns are not necessarily the same as their own. If trouble begins teachers often find themselves isolated from the support of colleagues.

- Secondly, although some people find themselves having to work alone for part of their lives by circumstance, many of those we have talked to chose to work alone out of preference: they like working alone and enjoy being their own bosses, not having to account and conform to others on a minute-by-minute basis.

- Thirdly, in spite of all the publicity that surrounds the accidents and attacks to Lone Workers, the majority of the Lone Worker's life is uneventful. Most of the time they are not falling down holes or being attacked by enraged house holders.

- Fourthly, and less happily, we find that virtually all of the Lone Workers we have talked to do not appear concerned with the dangers of serious incidents to themselves. They are, however, ready with at least second-hand stories of accidents, verbal abuse and physical attack, all of which have happened during assigned work.

We also find, in listening and questioning, that very basic precautions, preparations and training would have avoided the majority of incidents. 'I should have known' . . . and 'I was in a bit of a hurry and I didn't bother to . . .', are phrases attached to most of the horror stories. Unfortunately, precautions seem to be taken and training invoked as a response to an actual incident – fire fighting as opposed to fire prevention.

There is, however, a rump – the basically unavoidable incidents where a combination of circumstances conspire against the Lone Worker – and it is this rump that often makes the best Press stories. Even in these cases, which are very rare indeed, we see that basic precautions and training might have reduced the severity of the incident.

How this book came to be written

Our own involvement with the problems of the Lone Worker has been through our Assertiveness Training programmes and in particular with a series we developed for the National Rivers Authority in the North of England. The original training programmes were not targeted towards Lone Workers but were designed for a more general audience. Their content and balance were set after numerous discussions with employers and senior managers. Two quotations from employers were typical:

'Some of our people do not always act appropriately and in my view the issue is one of communication. Often with my staff I find them answering as they think I want them to respond and I don't get the true information I need from them. They are passive with an undue diffidence to my authority and I don't like that. They are paid to be experts and I need them to face up to me. I don't have time to tease it out of them.'

'I get complaints from the public that some of my staff are coming over as being arrogant. I talk to them about the specific incidents and I can only sympathise with the public – what my people have said and done would come over to me as being aggressive and certainly would have prevented me from being co-operative. In my view if you come over as aggressive, other people react that way to you and sometimes you get what you deserve.'

The first manager in our two examples was complaining about passive behaviour in his presence and the second about aggressive behaviour to the public – both behaviours, in the circumstances quoted, were inappropriate and, apart from blocking communication, could well put the staff at risk. Both excessively passive and aggressive people seem to invite aggression in others. Assertive people are more able to get on with the job and are less likely to stir up hostility in others – an issue of particular importance to Lone Workers. We began to see our workshops not just in terms of communication but also in terms of making jobs safer.

The philosophy behind the design of our programme was that assertive people communicate more easily and are able to work more professionally. *Our view is that the assertive person has a certain freedom – he or she is able to choose the most appropriate course of action and not move into a knee-jerk response when put under personal pressure.*

During our programmes we asked the participants to recall and work through situations where they found themselves acting inappropriately. Although many of the situations were examples of inappropriate passive or aggressive behaviour, some were not. They told us of potentially dangerous situations which were, in our view, caused by a lack of elementary planning and 'common sense'.

Listening to several such cases we remembered the case of Suzy Lamplugh who disappeared in 1986. It was natural, therefore, when we were commissioned by the National Rivers Authority in 1992 to run a series of one-day workshops for all their staff on 'safe working for Lone Workers', that we contacted Suzy's mother, Diana Lamplugh and The Suzy Lamplugh Trust. This book is the outcome.

The Suzy Lamplugh case

Many of us will already be aware, at least vaguely, of the Suzy Lamplugh case. Suzy worked as an estate agent and was last seen on 28 July 1986 at lunchtime, leaving a property she was attempting to sell in Sharrolds Road, Fulham. She was leaving with a client and was never seen again. According to her mother, Suzy was extremely confident in her work and abilities and in all ways felt equal to her male colleagues.

The Suzy Lamplugh story is told in a very personal and effective way by Diana Lamplugh in her book *Without Fear – The Key to Staying Safe*. The details of Suzy's last days will probably never be known, but what emerges is a very human story. In the book Diana lists the key areas where her daughter made mistakes – where she was less vigilant than the world in which she found herself demanded.

PRUDENT PRECAUTIONS

- Suzy only wrote down the man's name (Mr Kipper), not his address or telephone number, nor did she ring back to check the address was genuine.
- She did not take the man to the office, effectively logging herself and him in and out, and he could not therefore be identified by anyone.
- She did not take a companion with her into the empty house.

Suzy thought she could cope and wanted to prove that she could. Men and women can be caught from different ends of the necessity to be seen to be able to cope. For men the ability to cope is often seen as a demonstration of manhood. For women it may be seen as a demonstration of equality in a man's world. For a man or a woman having to prove one's ability to cope can be deadly.

Accepting safety procedures can well be tedious and unless *everyone* follows them *all* the time it may become the accepted procedure to ignore them. When this happens it somehow becomes an admission of inferiority to take precautions.

Procedures are tedious and probably unnecessary and unused on 99 out of 100 occasions. But it is the 100th that was the last for Suzy.

PRIOR WARNING SIGNS

Suzy may well have had numerous prior warning signals that the particular situation was dangerous and different. She may well have chosen to ignore them.

- Although we cannot ever be certain of the connection, Suzy had told her mother and the office staff that someone had been pestering her with annoying telephone calls.

There is a suggestion that the man subsequently known as Mr Kipper was threatening her in some way and that Suzy chose to ignore the increased risk in her job. Her work involved showing clients round empty properties and what might be an acceptable risk for a strong and assertive young woman in normal circumstances had become more risky because someone was pestering her. That someone could well be a 'client' asking to be shown round a vacant property.

A very common feature of 'incidents' is that the Lone Workers, for some reason, decide not to listen to the warning signals in their own heads and proceed with what they would do normally. We will never know exactly what Suzy knew and expected but she certainly had an inkling of potential trouble.

A CONFUSION OF OBJECTIVES

Suzy's job was to sell houses but she also wished to demonstrate her independence. She put herself at particular risk by showing a client around an empty property.

- Suzy's was a legitimate estate agency, selling property to prospective customers. Throughout the investigations of her disappearance there is the suggestion that she was trying to prove her ability to stand on her own two feet and tackle problems herself.

These are all very basic mistakes, but they are mistakes which can be avoided if we all become more aware of our own situations and the situations of those for whom we have responsibility. All of us, whatever trade or profession, whether we work alone or in crowded offices, are at risk from accidents, assaults and abuse as we go about our daily work. We obviously have moral and commercial obligations to take care of ourselves and our staff but we also have legal obligations. All managers and their staff have a legal obligation under common law and the Health and Safety at Work Act to take reasonable precautions related to the risk and the cost of those precautions. Further legislation is now in force from the EC. In the book we will discuss the very practical issues of lost time, morale and efficiency from what we may term 'incidents'. We will also discuss the very serious adverse publicity surrounding 'incidents'.

The content and structure of our book

Our belief is that understanding is the first step and our book is primarily about understanding. It is also about managers and individuals accepting responsibility. The contents of the book could be reduced to three rules – the basic rules of survival for Lone Workers:

1. **Be prepared**
2. **Be aware and take care**
3. **Be professional and do not confuse your objectives.**

However, life is not so simple. What we have written can be used as a survival kit for Lone Workers and their managers. As such it gives practical advice. As you read it we hope that the many exercises will help you relate what we are saying to your own situation.

Our purpose is for you, the Lone Workers and managers, to be able to:

- identify the potential risks;
- plan your own procedures for improved safety; and
- recognise the danger signs and cope accordingly.

But perhaps most importantly:

- get the most out of your chosen work without undue fear and allow others to do the same.

The book is intended to be a kit to help you, the Lone Worker, enjoy your chosen way of life and pursue it with minimum risk.

The first chapter looks at the Lone Worker's job and its motivations, a theme which is extended into Chapter 2. Both chapters discuss the important issues of managing Lone Workers most effectively but Chapter 2 introduces the issue of personal stress.

The third chapter is about the legal implications of accidents and violent incidents and the procedures that need to be taken both by the workers themselves and their managers to reduce the risks and the worries that they cause. At the end of the chapter readers are invited to prepare relevant safety procedures for their own jobs.

Chapter 4 considers the particular traps, personal and situational, that Lone Workers may find themselves in. We will look first at the question of mixed objectives and see how we can plan our jobs for the maximum enjoyment and safety. We will then go beyond planning and look at personal and organisational conduct that can reduce risk.

Chapter 5 considers the whole issue of aggression and violence. We will discuss how situations and people can move from a 'safe' or placid state to one of potential or actual risk.

Chapters 6 and 7 will look at how we, by our behaviours or attitudes, can contribute *to making problem situations*. We look at all the components of the way we present ourselves and our attitudes to other people and how we may best encourage others to act reasonably towards us.

Chapter 8 discusses what individual Lone Workers and their managers can do to both reduce stress levels to a useful level and cope with the stresses arising from assaults – verbal or physical.

Most of what we have discussed so far is common sense and we see our role as being that of helpers who have attempted to get the reader's thoughts into order and prepared him or her into action. In Chapter 9 we will deal with controversial issues: should Lone Workers be trained in martial arts or at least elementary self-defence, or is this inviting more serious trouble? (There are very well argued cases in each direction.); are certain types of Lone Worker jobs intrinsically unsafe and thus unsuitable for some individuals or groups?

One expressed view is that the presumed equality of the sexes means just that – women should be treated no differently from men regardless of the obvious issues. An alternative view is that if employers feel that women are especially at risk and that to employ them in certain areas would involve additional costs or extra effort, is it more efficient to employ men? Another view is that if certain jobs are intrinsically dangerous then *nobody* should be asked to do them without very special precautions. The reality may well lie between these views but the social consequences of the resolution of the argument are very large indeed. The appendices contains questionnaires, specimen forms, an example of a training programme and sources of help and assistance.

1

What does being a Lone Worker mean?

Introducing Alan and Barbara – The Lone Worker Job Profile Questionnaire – The job, the environment and the job holder – Meeting individual psychological needs – Working Needs Questionnaire.

Introducing Alan and Barbara

Alan recognised Barbara as she came into the station buffet. They had been in the same class at school but had never been close. Alan liked his own company and Barbara was always part of a gang – 'one of the girls'. Alan would have preferred to sit by himself but he was, at first, perfectly happy to reminisce socially and fill in the time between trains.

After trying to remember the names of teachers and the dates of various incidents they moved forward to what they had done after leaving school. Alan and Barbara had both worked in a variety of jobs before settling down into what they both saw as careers. By coincidence they were now both working in the same industry – insurance. Alan was on the road as an insurance agent and Barbara was in a small team selling directly to the public from the ground floor of a branch office.

Barbara's main job was to deal with insurance quotation requests and she had her own computer terminal. She bubbled on that she had been sent on a training course on customer relations and was beginning to be able to handle the other problems and issues that the customers brought to the counter.

Sadly she explained that: 'Being new to the business I still have to refer most of the odd problems to the others. They have been there longer, but I am learning. They are all very nice.'

The team leader was also available in the background to deal with 'even odder problems'. One such 'odder problem' had been a drunk causing a nuisance. Her boss had called the police to have the drunk ejected. It had evidently been quite a scene.

Alan did not say much but when Barbara brought up the incident with the drunk he remembered a similar incident the previous week when he was working in an urban housing estate. Working alone there had been no boss to emerge from the backroom, telephone in hand – Alan had had to handle it himself.

When his own train was announced Barbara was detailing what had been a fantastic Christmas party and Alan was relieved to get away. The more she had gone on about her job the more he realised that he would regard what she seemed to relish as a nightmare – working as part of a team to strict hours with the hurly burly of an open-plan office. Even hearing about the trials and tribulations of office life drained him. He settled into his seat and relaxed gradually with his crossword. The journey would take him two hours and he planned to use the last hour to complete his monthly report and get himself another cup of tea. He was coming home from the yearly meeting of all the agents and he had found the experience almost as exhausting as listening to Barbara; he would be glad to get back to his own patch.

Alan's job as an insurance agent was to obtain regular payments from a number of clients in their homes and at their business premises. Usually the money was ready for him but very occasionally he had to get tough and demand payment. As part of his job he also sold more insurance on a commission basis.

Each morning he would plan his day to cover his portfolio of calls. He designed the route for the minimum distance but he allowed himself some latitude in the order he made the calls and, in particular, putting the calls he thought would be most stressful towards, but not necessarily at, the end of the day. The route was also planned so that he had a convenient place for lunch and he could be reasonably near home for his last call – preferably with a client with whom he was friendly so that he was not strapped for time if the work element moved towards the social. On most days he would telephone the Head Office from home and leave his daily log on the answering service or fax.

Every Friday he attended a progress meeting and compared notes with the other agents. The meeting invariably closed for a beer and a general get together with smaller groups separating for exchanges of personal information and support. Alan himself was having some trouble at home and he knew that his colleagues, Bob or Susan, would be a helpful ear.

THE LONE WORKER JOB PROFILE QUESTIONNAIRE

Read the following six statements and decide how relevant they are to your own job.

	Very true	True sometimes	Not true
In my job, belonging to a team is not very important.	☐	☐	☐
Provided I do what is required, I am able to structure my day.	☐	☐	☐
When the unexpected occurs, it's basically up to me to sort it out.	☐	☐	☐
Within certain and normally well-understood guidelines, I am expected to make decisions.	☐	☐	☐
Although I have a base, my office is really some informal place – a car, a café, a train, etc.	☐	☐	☐
I meet the public, usually by myself, face to face.	☐	☐	☐

Barbara would find none of the statements in The Lone Worker Job Profile Questionnaire completely true.

- Working as an integrate team member was essential: she would have to understand at least part of everybody's jobs and stand-in for them when required. Her dress and general behaviour would have to 'fit in'.
- Her day began at 8.45am when the office was prepared for the onrush of clients and ended at 5pm when the doors were closed. She had a lunch break from 12.45pm to 1.30pm. If business allowed she and the others had coffee from the machine when they first came in and at about 11.00am and 3.30pm.
- As a new member of the team she was expected to refer any problems to the others in the team. The office and its organisation was designed to avoid the unexpected but, should it occur, others were brought in to help. The first line of help was immediate colleagues and then the boss who was able to bring in further resources – Head Office, the Police, etc.
- Ideally everything was reduced to computer systems and Barbara's own latitude to make decisions and choices was very limited indeed.
- Barbara worked in a formal office.
- Although meeting the public face to face, albeit separated by a counter, she was never 'alone'. Should anyone or anything get nasty, she had support.

Alan would be able to accept the basic truth of all six statements.

- Although the management called Alan's group a team, it was so only in the loosest sense. Alan was paid to do a job and whether that job was done or not done was his personal responsibility – up to a point. He knew his 'patch' and it would be very difficult for anyone to cover for him. There were no team norms – again up to a point. Alan could dress as he pleased, although a suit was obligatory. When he thought of his group at the last Friday meeting he remembered a range of anoraks, duffle coats, British Warms,

WHAT DOES BEING A LONE WORKER MEAN?

Barbours and even Columbo macs, hanging in the cloakroom. In Barbara's office there were three other women and two men. They all wore uniforms – white shirt and tie with blue trousers for the men and white blouse and scarf for the women with blue skirts. It had been a joke that Barbara, who had joined the office with short hair, would have to grow her's to match the other women's long tresses. Both the men had short hair.

- Alan, as we have already said, planned his own day. He arranged his portfolio of visits on certain personal criteria – a good place to eat lunch and a convenient place to finish, difficult clients interspersed with people he enjoyed meeting and talking to.

- The unexpected came in two guises for Alan. He had been working for ten years in the industry, although for several employers, and very little surprised him. But changes in the law did mean that he had to get occasional guidance from Head Office and, surprisingly less often, from his boss. Much more important examples of the unexpected came from his clients – tears instead of anger when he had to enforce payments, and open aggression when he expected to be thanked.

Quite recently he had, as he thought, helped a single parent family by restructuring their insurance. The previous scheme was designed to cover the possible unemployment of the ex-husband and was, in Alan's view, too expensive and did not fit the new situation. When Alan returned the revised documents he was met with the woman's new partner who resented Alan's interference. He resented Alan's interference to the extent of backing Alan against a wall and punching him in the mouth. It was one of the few times when Alan regretted not having the support of a nice full office and the protection of a counter.

- Apart from planning his day, Alan made hundreds of work-related decisions every week. The broad strategy was laid down but Alan knew that he was judged by getting the money in. Sometimes that meant coming back later or even on occasion minding the kids for a client while they borrowed the money from a neighbour. On one occasion when a family was in temporary trouble, he even acted as a sort of pawnbroker. He was quite aware that the company policy would not support him when he acted on his own initiative but experience told him that it worked. He got his money and sold extra policies.

- Alan's office was his car, his home, various forms of public transport and, as he joked to one boss, a car park in Birkenhead.

In a previous job Alan had been a sales representative selling shoes and he had to report his weekly figures to the office on Thursday evening. He was equipped with a hand-held computer and every Thursday evening he parked next to the telephone box in the supermarket carpark and calculated his weekly returns. He then plugged in the computer modem to the public telephone and phoned up later to clarify details. For Alan, in this job, the car was very much his office.

- Alan's contacts with the public were, if at all possible, face to face, although occasionally separated by a front door. Trouble, in the short term, was his own problem.

Alan, by our definition, is a true Lone Worker. Postal delivery workers, journalists, taxi drivers, service engineers, Pollution Control Officers, Social Workers, etc., may all qualify for the title to a greater or lesser extent.

The job, the environment and the job holder

Some jobs are normally better done, regardless of any other factors, by people working alone. One such example is writing. We accept that several successful writers work in pairs but there is always a danger of clashing – roles are not defined, creative egos brush each other, credit may be seen to be unfairly spread. Salespeople too may well find that it is easier and more effective to establish a relationship without a partner present. The qualified service engineer may resent having to explain what he or she is doing to a less able assistant when the pressure is on.

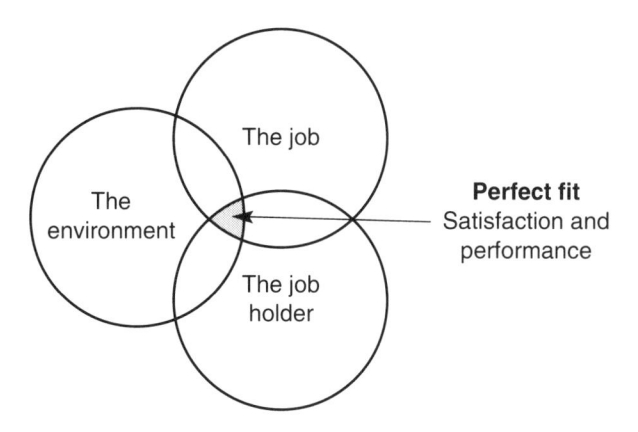

Figure 1.1 The perfect job

The business or working *environment* may well require that some jobs are to be done alone. Economic grounds may make it unjustifiable to provide more than one person on a job, even if it means that the job takes that much longer. For example, postal delivery workers might find it easier and perhaps quicker if they worked in pairs, sharing the weight of the delivery and reducing the distance travelled by 'leap frogging' to households. It might be quicker but one suspects that additional cost would not be universally justified. One-man buses have many disadvantages but are justified on cost grounds alone. Some working conditions dictate sole working. For instance, it is difficult to see how more than one person could get into the booths used for selling lottery tickets.

The final factor is the job holder and his or her own psychological make-up. People differ and want different things from the workplace. *The 'perfect job' for an individual working in the real world is where these three factors overlap – the job holder, his or her environment and the job itself (see* Fig. 1.1*).*

We need to look further at this and will provide the reader with an opportunity to check on his or her own psychological needs from the workplace. Before we do this, however, we need to look at how the three factors interrelate.

The *environment,* in its overall sense, shapes the job and to a lesser extent, for most jobs, the job shapes the environment. Consider Barbara and the way that economic, technical and social pressures have created what we have called the 'insurance shop'. Barbara's forerunners would have worked in a closed office with little or no direct contact with the public. The high spot of the day would be opening the mail and most of the time would have been spent on typing and answering telephone calls. The application of the computer to most aspects of the business is certainly one reason for the changes, but not the only one. Businesses that survive, recognise changes in the environment and adapt what they do accordingly. In a less fundamental way, the job and the way people do it, changes the environment, locally and globally. The office will be structured so that there is an element of privacy while the clients are guided through the computer screened questions. The site of the office will be in a shopping precinct and not in a business area.

The interactions between the *job holder* and the *job* are equally complex. Again looking a Barbara's job, we will have found that when the initial decision was made to open the insurance 'shop', some of the office staff who had previously sold insurance over the telephone, were unsuitable for direct customer contact and those that stayed with the company were retained in the more traditional environment. The requirement to work with computers will also have affected who went and who stayed. Once established, the company will recruit people who have or have the aptitude to be trained in the core skills of customer relations and computer literacy and the personality of someone who likes to work in a team.

However well the jobs in Barbara's office are specified, the job holders will shape and modify the environment and the job itself. An example of this occurred before Barbara joined the team. Charles, who had some previous experience with computers, found himself an unofficial troubleshooter for technical problems. This role he enjoyed and developed. Over the months he was given less and less direct customer contact and his desk was moved to a more suitable place for providing technical advice to the rest of the team.

Given the opportunity, we work to our strengths. An example of this is how Alan got his job as a Lone Worker – the insurance agent – in the first place. He was recruited initially as an insurance clerk. A very small part of his job, and the jobs of everyone else in the office, was the occasional visit to check on dubious claims in his portfolio of clients. He liked this side of the business and began to take on visits for other people. On one of his trips away from the office he met an insurance agent for another company and they compared jobs. What Alan heard about the agent's work appealed and he applied for the job he is now doing and enjoying. The job of the insurance agent – the Lone Worker job – met his psychological needs and allowed him to use the skills that he himself valued.

There are as many ways of describing motivation as there are management books about the subject. Here we are saying that we are motivated by jobs that:

- meet our psychological needs; and
- allow us to play to our strengths in skills, aptitudes and knowledge.

The manager who wishes to have motivated staff needs to match the job holders, the job and the environment so that individual psychological needs are met and the skills that individuals value can be used.

The Alans of this world value personal independence and do not require to belong to a tightly integrated team. They are Lone Workers from choice. The Barbaras of this world *need* to have people around them and thus are comfortable working in teams. Teams fulfil their psychological needs and although, on occasion, most of us need to work by ourselves, it is not by choice and we are grateful to get back to the group.

WORKING ALONE

Meeting individual psychological needs

WHY DO PEOPLE WORK IN THE FIRST PLACE?

Job satisfaction is about fulfilling basic human needs, and for any individual the balance of these needs is very important. However casual we may seem to be about our work, the job itself provides for at least some of our needs: most people like to be able to measure success, to have the satisfaction of making something, or to see a result for their efforts. All these satisfactions are concerned with us using the skills, aptitudes and knowledge we value. Beyond this we *all* also have needs concerned with relating to the rest of the human race.

THE JOB AND COMPANIONSHIP

The way people need to relate to the rest of the human race is very personal. Barbara, when she talked to Alan about her job was very much concerned with belonging to a team – relating to people *en masse*. She was also concerned with her status in the team – training, referring to more experienced colleagues and having intimates with whom she can share her problems and aspirations. The job she does is important and she is proud of her ability to use the computer and give advice. However, it is the people side of her work that really excites her.

Alan too derived satisfaction from the job but seems much less concerned with either belonging to a team or status. He likes to work within a clear situation and mentions particular individuals with whom he has close relations at work.

Our point is that the balance of Barbara's human needs – essential ingredients to a fully functioning Barbara – is satisfied by her job and the team. Alan has quite a different balance of human needs and these too are satisfied by his job. There is no promise that Barbara and Alan will stay with their personal balances, but at this moment in time, this is the balance they enjoy and these are two types of job that most satisfy that balance.

The Working Needs Questionnaire is a simplification of a test that can be given when testing the suitability of individuals to working alone and jobs that require that ability.

WORKING NEEDS QUESTIONNAIRE

We have filled the questionnaire in for Barbara and Alan, leaving a column for you, the reader, to complete. You have 10 points to allocate between each set of questions.

Question 1

When you arrive at the office or place of work do you:

	Barbara's score	Alan's score	Reader's score
(a) want to get straight down to work?	0	2	
(b) find out what everyone has been doing?	6	0	
(c) check out whether people have done what you asked for?	1	4	
(d) have an informal chat with a colleague?	3	2	

Question 2

When you are invited to a 'firms' party do you:

(a) think it is probably all part of the job but hope for a suitable excuse to avoid it?	0	8	
(b) look forward to seeing everyone?	5	0	
(c) remember that you are organising at least part of it anyway?	2	0	
(d) look forward to meeting some old friends?	3	2	

WORKING ALONE

Question 3

When you are moved and have to work with a new group of people do you:

	Barbara's score	Alan's score	Reader's score
(a) get into a corner and start work while they argue?	0	4	
(b) worry whether you will fit in?	2	0	
(c) attempt to establish order or hope that somebody will tell you exactly what is required of you?	7	2	
(d) look around for friendly or familiar faces?	1	4	

Question 4

If you were sent away on a long training course would you:

	Barbara's score	Alan's score	Reader's score
(a) hope that the jobs you have left will be completed properly?	0	6	
(b) feel that you may be left out of the action when you come back?	4	1	
(c) make regular checks while you are away?	0	2	
(d) ask one or two people to let you know if something really important turns up and you need to know?	6	2	

Question 5

If you were asked to present your work at a conference would you:

	Barbara's score	Alan's score	Reader's score
(a) concentrate on the written presentation – handouts, visual aids, etc.?	3	5	
(b) concentrate on the oral presentation and how you present yourself – clothes, hair style, etc.?	7	1	
(c) get involved in the organisation?	0	0	
(d) look forward to the questions and in particular the informal discussions after your paper has been presented?	0	4	

Now add up the scores for (a), (b), (c) and (d) – the maximum score would be 50. See how you have scored below:

0 to 5 is low: this factor does not reflect any major need. Conversely, the personal needs are so low that they are easily satisfied and the person concerned may become exhausted should it appear in excess. (Alan, we will remember, who has a low need to belong to groups, became tired when Barbara 'gushed' over him in the station buffet.)

6 to 15 is medium: this need to belong factor is important but unlikely to define behaviour.

16 < is high: such a score represents a major need which is likely to be reflected in both day-to-day behaviour and in job choice.

When we look at the relative scores of (a), (b), (c) and (d) we are looking at personal targets for the balance that makes the job side of our life satisfying. The (a) scores are about the human needs provided by the job itself. The (b), (c) and (d) scores are about our needs in relation to others; (b) is about our need to belong; (c) is about our need to have clarity in our relationships with others; and (d) is about our need to communicate with others on an intimate level. The ideal jobs for us meet the balance of factors which our personalities demand – not too little or too much.

If we look at the scores for Alan and Barbara we can see some patterns. The total for (a) is about concern for the task. Alan has a score of 25 and Barbara 3. The score of 25 is high and reflects both Alan's behaviour and his choice of career. We may see this as one reason why Alan chooses to work on his own – he wants to get on with the job whereas *any* companion is likely to require some non-job related effort which Alan is not prepared to give.

Alan's main concern is very much for the job itself and his managers will need to understand this. If, for any reason, Alan finds the job impossible or that he is dissatisfied with his own performance, then Alan will become demotivated. The ideal way of managing anyone with a high (a) score is to discuss with them as an equal the elements of the operation of the task, especially if the task is to undergo changes. Alan's manager should:

- show a real interest in the operational aspects of the job and consult Alan about these should any changes be envisaged;
- set clear guidelines for the job and not interfere unless absolutely necessary in 'how the job is actually done'; and
- accept that Alan is an individual and not force him to relate socially to others.

Barbara has a low score for (a) – the *task*-related factor. This does not mean that she is not a professional who is concerned with results and effective performance. It does, however, indicate that she is more concerned with the people with whom she works and how she relates to them. The *people* factors – (b), (c) and (d) – are the determining factors of her job satisfaction. For Barbara it is with whom she works, and not what she does, that is more important. If she does not relate to the people in her team she will be unhappy and either leave or perform well below her potential.

The individual (b) scores relate to the needs all of us have, to some measure, of belonging and relating to others – relating to the human race in general and to the particular groups or teams within which we function.

Alan has a very low (b) score – only 2, whereas Barbara has a high score – 24. Alan is, as he has already told us, happy in his own company. Alan not only does not need the company of others to a high degree but when presented with the noise of people in quantity, becomes exhausted. He has the typical profile of some one who is a Lone Worker by choice. However, Barbara, with her high score, is indicating that she *needs* the company of others to function effectively. Because of the level of this need she would find any job where she was isolated from others as being completely demotivating.

Managing and motivating people with low (b) score involves *not* expecting them to attend unnecessary group meetings.

Where a general get together is absolutely necessary it must be structured round the task and permit informal discussions outside the mass meeting. People with high belonging needs have to be reminded on a fairly continuous basis that they are part of a team. They welcome group activities some of which may seem patronising to people such as Alan.

The (c) scores are about needing to have a defined role in relationships with others. Both Barbara and Alan have medium scores – Alan 8 and Barbara 11. Both need some imposed structure in their lives and both of them need imposed boundaries within which they will work effectively. In a completely loose structure – 'go out and find some clients, anywhere will do' – they will use their energies to define structures before getting down to work. A high (c) score indicates that individuals have a high need for a defined role – he or she need to know exactly where they are and may well take a dictatorial lead in certain circumstances. Low scores are indicators of people who very much want to go their own way: they neither wish to dominate nor be dominated; they may have enough self-confidence so that they do not need to measure themselves against others, or so little that they blow with the wind.

The manager wishing to motivate medium or high scorers in (c) – the role factor – need to impose a formal structure: job definition, reporting procedures, hierarchy, etc., and allow an informal structure to develop. The secret is one of careful observation and correction should the informal structures fail to meet the organisation's overall objectives. We may remember the way in which the computer buff in Barbara's office redefined his job. Managers need to be aware that the process of job restructuring is inevitable if the team and individuals are to remain motivated but also remain in overall control. The job redefinition *must* remain within the overall job demands.

The (d) scores indicate a need for one-to-one relationships. Both Alan and Barbara have medium scores – 14 and 15 respectively. Looking at the scores in context, Alan values relationships with individuals as opposed to groups. Barbara has a score of 15 for values and needs relationships with groups *and* individuals.

Typically we find that certain groups of specialists *claim* low scores on (d). These are very private people who are very selective in their company. We have met specialists who have low scores on (b), (c) and (d). Managing such people presents a creative challenge to management.

A major multinational engaged a computer specialist to design packaging for a range of liquid products. The problem was to optimise consumer appeal, supermarket shelf prominence, strength in distribution and cost of manufacture.

The man was impossible to manage in any accepted sense. He worked in great spurts – 48 hours at a time – and then retreated into himself for weeks on end. His dedication and creativity was astounding and his ultimate achievements justified any level of expenditure. The problem was compounded by his lack of English.

This, the ultimate Lone Worker, was given a specially customised flat near the computer centre of the organisation. The flat housed the specialist and his young family. Beyond the 'home' area of the flat there was the working area, set up with access to such computer power as he needed and which could be used entirely at his discretion.

In the chapters that follow we will not be considering the problems, concerns and opportunities of working as or with 'the ultimate Lone Worker'. We will be discussing the problems, concerns and opportunities of ordinary men and women who by choice or by circumstance find themselves working alone. In the next chapter we will look at the issue of people who enjoy working alone.

2

The enjoyment of working alone

*The 'bears and squares' – The FRAME principle of job boundaries –
The Lone Worker and self motivation – Stress and the Lone Worker –
Stress and the balance of 'people needs' – Support mechanisms.*

The 'bears and squares'

Diana Lamplugh describes the children's game of 'bears and squares' as a metaphor to develop the issues of working alone and enjoying working alone. The game, along with 'Pooh Sticks', was first given to the adult world by A.A. Milne in his Christopher Robin stories. To start playing the game of 'bears and squares' the child needs a pavement with slabs wide enough to walk on. The object of the game is to keep to the squares. Once you tread on the lines between them 'the bears will get you'. The bears lurked round every bend. Thousands of children will have invented variations of the square-hopping game, and as they hopped happily across the paving slabs they would hope that nobody, particularly the 'bears', would notice if they strayed on to the odd line.

Alan, and other Lone Workers from choice, enjoy working in the squares which represent areas of their own cherished responsibility. In the squares they can feel safe and are their own bosses. The lines represent a frame of outside control and the wise Lone Worker remains constantly aware of its presence. The most obvious, but not the only 'lines', are determined by 'the employer', whether the employer is an organisation or a customer.

For Alan the frame that encloses his job consists of certain core rules: he *must* visit all his clients regularly, be completely trustworthy and keep good records. These rules define the scope of his job and the frame within which he needs to operate and still remain employed. We are not saying that there are not other elements in Alan's job, but what we are saying is that if he does *not* fulfil any one of the three core elements, he will be in serious trouble – he will have strayed outside his frame and on to one of the 'lines'. There will be other non-core rules in his job and with these he has some discretion.

In any job there are certain core rules – the MUSTS – and certain non-core rules – the NEEDs

Working within these core rules Alan has a great deal of freedom – he is virtually master of his own fate.

A wise employer will make the core rules that frame a job clear. The core rules should be about what Alan *has* to do and not about the way Alan *should* do it. Alan and every other Lone Worker derive their satisfaction from *'doing it my way'* – the skill of the employer is defining what is meant by *'it'*.

The core rules of a job are the **FRAME** within which the job holder works.

> **Few** – we do not want a long list. It is usual to able to reduce a job to three or four core rules.
>
> **Realistic** – there must be no wishful thinking about the core rules. The job holder must be able to work within the frame *all* the time.
>
> **Agreed,** accepted and communicated – each job holder must know what is expected and not rely on hearsay. He or she must accept the core rules.
>
> **Monitored** – the 'bears' need to be watchful. Because of their nature any slackness in applying the core rules is serious for both the 'employer' and the job holder. It is profoundly de-

motivating to find that while *we* have stuck to the rules, *others* are able to break them with impunity.

Essential – they must be seen to be what they are, i.e. the frame within which the job exists. Working within the frame the job holder has personal freedom. Working outside the frame the job is like any other.

In our metaphor, as Alan grew more confident and competent his slabs became larger but the bears were still minding the lines. The FRAME was still in place, but the non-core rules were slackened and his personal freedom grew. Thus, when Alan started the job the rules of dress were strictly applied as was the rule that he had to report back to the office each day. As Alan grew to be the most experienced operator in the office it became accepted *informally* that he was allowed to wear clothes of his own choice provided they were smart. He also gained the privilege of only having to report to the office in person once a week.

In any set of rules the employer needs a process of constant review of core rules, as indeed of all rules. Rules, it has been said, are made to be broken. However by their very nature core rules are absolute for any moment in time. The job of a manager is to understand which of the rules *are* core and to maintain solidly these rules. The sensible Lone Worker keeps within the frame of the core rules and enjoys autonomy. What we may call secondary rules are the bargaining pieces that the manager may allow to be modified by the Lone Worker as a tool for increased motivation.

Instructions to Lone Workers should be WHATS and not HOWS.

- **WHATS allow Lone Workers scope for job development and motivation.**
- **HOWS, for all but the most inexperienced, are at best restrictive and at worst completely demotivating.**

When in doubt, err on the side of the simple and few.

All rules are made for a purpose. Always be aware of the purpose and be willing to check challenges to the rules against that purpose.

Exercise 2.1

Consider the rules that you as a Lone Worker, or you as an employer of Lone Workers, lay down. List the core rules. These are the lines in our metaphor that separate the squares within which the Lone Worker operates.

What is the purpose of the job itself? Are all the core rules relevant to the purpose and if not, review the rules that somehow say more about the prejudices of the past of the organisation than the present. Are they Few, Realistic, Agreed, Monitorable and Essential? Do they fit our FRAME?

What are the 'secondary rules'? Which of the 'secondary rules' can be used as a motivational reward to 'experienced' Lone Workers?

The Lone Worker and self-motivation

For many Lone Workers the major motivations are *not* having to conform to standards of behaviour set by colleagues and being away from immediate supervisory control. In Alan's case we may remember how Alan was able to structure his job so that his schedule of visits allowed him to have his lunch stop at favourite sites. Alan would also arrange his schedule to allow time to talk to particular friends and perhaps stay with them for a cup of tea. This did not mean that Alan worked less hard or that 'he strayed on to the lines' – he always completed his calls, never flawed his collections and reported effectively. However, he structured his work and this structuring was his principal satisfaction.

Occasionally Head Office insisted that he took a trainee on his rounds and he invariably found this an intrusion. Working alone he could be grumpy or happy when *he* felt like it and his only professional face was that required by the job. He did not have to adjust his behaviour to suit colleagues and this he saw as the reason he preferred working alone and not as part of a team. Alan accepted that others – and here he would think of

Barbara – actually needed the control of working in a team, he did not. Alan liked to set his own norms and standards of behaviour.

THE MASLOW THEORY OF SELF-MOTIVATION

Maslow believed that human needs form a type of hierarchy, so that normally a lower level need has to be at least partially satisfied before a higher level is pursued.

The levels of the Maslow hierarchy are shown in Fig 2.1. Only when individuals have fulfilled their basic, physiological needs (food, shelter, warmth, etc.) will they seek a higher level of need, for example, acceptance by a particular social group.

In our example of a Lone Worker, Alan has low 'belonging' and social needs. These needs do exist for him but they are not a prime factor in his motivation. We would expect his prime motivations to be in Esteem and what Maslow, a notable lecturer and writer on management theory, called self-actualisation – doing his own thing as we have already discussed – which are higher up the hierarchy. He may well surprise his bosses by being concerned with status and worry significantly about the car he is given and how he is recognised at the company social occasions he attends.

Alan's self-actualisation within the job may not be enough and research reveals that many Lone Workers set themselves little tasks while they work. The 'little tasks' could well be dismissed as silly games but they provide sub-targets that can enliven dull periods and provide genuine motivation.

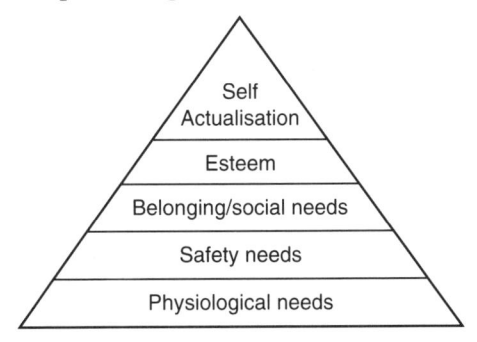

Figure 2.1 The Maslow hierarchy

Alan, for instance, might set himself silly exercises. While driving to a distant client he might attempt to do *exactly* 30 miles an hour between measured distances. He might set himself an exact time for a particular visit or set up 'records' for a set of visits. These, if he were challenged, would be totally silly exercises but they would still be a part of his motivation. Alan would always be aware that 'exercises' were a game and should anything unusual happen, they would be dropped immediately. There was no way that Alan was going to walk on a 'line' or break the core rules of his job and move outside the frame.

Once Alan had decided that he wanted to listen to the whole of a play on the radio without interruptions. To do this he had to complete his morning schedule of calls ten minutes faster than his previous record. Up to 11 o'clock he was slightly behind his target time but he was still confident of reaching his personally imposed target.

The next call was to an old-age pensioner who always had the money ready for him in an envelope by the door and he hoped make up further time on the last three calls by using the new ring road. As he climbed the steps to the pensioner's flat he knew something was wrong and he met the ambulance-man in the doorway. His client had just been found dead and all thought of the 'record' vanished.

As we have discussed, every job has certain core elements. Alan's core job elements are a need to visit all his clients, to be trustworthy and keep good records. It was the record-keeping that delayed him so considerably with the death of the pensioner. Without a thought, Alan would abandon his 'games' and become once again a professional.

Exercise 2.2

If you are a Lone Worker, think of the 'little exercises' you set yourself to maintain your interest. How important are these in your 'job satisfaction'? Do the games interfere, or have the potential of interfering, with your core job?

Stress and the Lone Worker

Most of us require some form of stress to work effectively. There is, even on holiday, a very fine line between relaxation and boredom, and stress can be truly invigorating. However, when we talk of stress we are usually discussing the negative form of stress – the stress that is actually disabling.

The line between the positive and negative – the invigorating and disabling – forms of stress can be narrow and very personal. On a 'good day' we can feel that we can handle anything, but on a 'bad day' the slightest deviation from our planned world can set us behaving in a dysfunctional way. Chapter 8 will deal with stress in more detail and propose how negative stress can be avoided.

The stage at which positive stimulation turns into unhealthy stress is different for all of us. Our personality, behaviour and lifestyle all have important influences on our stress levels. Some people thrive on pressure whereas others find it overwhelming. Stress only becomes harmful when we cannot control our responses to it. Recognising this is the first step to learning how to manage and reduce the harmful effects of stress.

As you look at the Fig. 2.2, picture at which point on the curve you are at the present moment. Do you need more stimulation in your life to improve your efficiency or do you need to take stock of the situation, cut out the unnecessary activities that are crammed into your life and start saying 'NO' to extra work? Ask yourself several times a day, 'at what point on the curve am I at this moment in time?' You will find that it varies.

For the Lone Worker, as for any human being, coping with stress is essential for both physical health and effective performance. Knowing yourself is a vital prerequisite to being able to manage pressure successfully. How else will you know how much you can take on? To make the most of pressure you need to be aware of the messages coming from your body, for example how tired or tense you feel. You must also be aware of how you react to situations, and ensure that you remain objective and act in a rational and appropriate way.

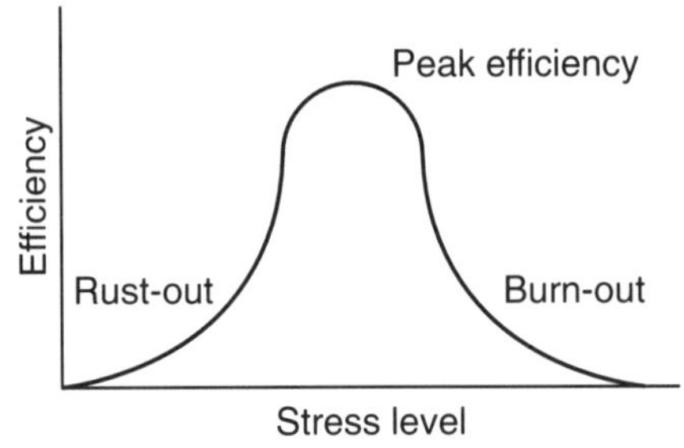

Figure 2.2 Stress and efficiency

Psychologists have identified two broad personality types, one of which is more prone to stress than the other. 'Type A' is the notorious stress-prone personality whose typical behaviour and lifestyle constantly elicit physical arousal. Type As are impatient, ambitious, competitive, aggressive, and hard working; they set high goals and demands of themselves and others and they are particularly prone to anxiety. 'Type Bs', on the other hand, have a reverse profile. They are equable, calm, relaxed, not overtly ambitious, and less at risk from stress and heart disease. Few of us possess all the characteristics of either type. In general our personality is made up of a preponderance of one or other patterns of behaviour, or, in rare cases, a perfect balance of both. Recognising situations when our stress-prone traits emerge helps to protect us from stress. Questionnaires to help you assess your stress levels are given in Appendix 3.

Our insurance agent, Alan, was able to let off steam at the regular monthly meetings with his colleagues, but from a day-to-day basis he had no one with whom to relate. He had targets to reach, which sometimes meant having to work nights and weekends, and he had awkward customers to deal with, yet he still had to be polite because 'the customer is always right'. However, he had no office staff to shout at when he had had a bad day. He didn't have anyone standing over him to tell him what, when and how to do a job, nor praise from a supervisor when he had achieved it. This will all contribute to the pressure put on Alan as a Lone Worker.

Exercise 2.3

First it would be useful for you to write down the day-to-day events which you feel put you under pressure or that you do not like doing. Our list would contain items such as:

- *using the car on a cold and damp morning;*
- *doing the VAT returns; and*
- *delivering training courses.*

While none of these poses a real life threat each one pushes higher up the stress curve.

LOSS OF EMPOWERMENT

Freud saw our lives as being a battle between two Gods – Eros and Thanatos. Eros stands for *disorder*, change, creativity, newness, challenge, excitement – things outside our or others' control. Thanatos stands for *order*, regularity, standards, certainty – things controlled by us or others.

As human beings we set our own balance between Eros and Thanatos (see Fig. 2.3) – for our whole lives and not just for our world of work. If our lives at work have been particularly chaotic and we feel that we have lost personal control, then we demand more control, stability and harmony from our home and leisure life. In this way we can restore the balance. For Barbara, working in the 'controlled' world of the office, her

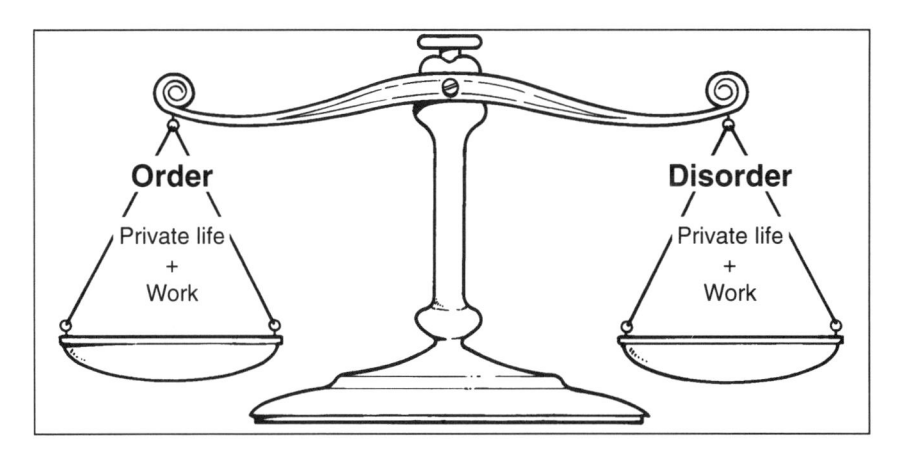

Figure 2.3 A personal balance between order and disorder

private life may well provide much of her excitement. We suspect, however, that Barbara needs less excitement overall than Alan. Alan, although needing more uncertainty overall, will still need a measure of certainty and order. He will seek to be in control of the balance. If he finds things getting out of control at work he will rely more on his home and private life to provide what he may well call *stability*.

Alan has his own strategy for handling a hard day on the road. His wife also has a job and the children are normal, unpredictable and demanding. Disorder is the norm at home, a state which Alan loves on a good day. On a 'bad day' when things have not gone as he planned he will ring home and arrange to take his wife out for a meal where others can deal with the uncertainties and he can restore his own personal balance of order and disorder.

Exercise 2.4

Think of an 'ideal' day and what happens to give you personal stress. As an example, we have listed the sort of things that 'wound Alan up' – things that caused him a bad day.

Alan would start the day with cherished routines – washing, cleaning his teeth, reading the paper, doing the Quick Crossword, listening to the coffee percolating . . . *Then the phone would ring asking him to check into the office to meet a visitor. His planned schedule had gone.*

He would finish the toast and get into the car. *The starter whirls and the engine dies . . .*

He would check into the office to meet the visitor and collect the schedule for the day – prepared yesterday . . . *There is a note that Fred is off sick and Alan has to cover some of his urgent calls as well as his own.*

On the motorway well on schedule . . . *The red tail lights ahead indicate a blockage. After about an hour of stop–go motoring the entire revised schedule has gone. To make matters worse when he got moving there is no sign of any reason for the delay.*

The day we have described is familiar to the writers and is what we would call stressful. Stress for us is about losing control, or about not being master of our own fate. For us our own planning efficiency seems, on a bad day, to encourage other people to devise ingenious ways of changing the rules. What makes a bad day for you?

Stress is about loss of empowerment – the inability to determine the balance of our own lives.

Stress and the balance of 'people needs'

Being able to command self-autonomy is the essence of the Lone Worker's driving force and losing this self-autonomy is stressful in itself. The example we quoted about Alan's 'bad day' was about his inability to define his own world, within the frame he had chosen to live. We plan stability to our own formula of excitement against predictability and *others* refuse to accept our plan. The random telephone call, the flat battery and the traffic jam conspire to beat our plans, disturb our balance and put us under pressure.

Pressure leads to stress which, up to a point, is probably a good thing.

Most of us require some form of pressure to work effectively.

However we all have limits, and the limits are determined by our whole life and not just our working life.

Our total lives need a balance of order and disorder. The Lone Worker has chosen a path where he or she demands what, probably to others, is a high degree of autonomy in the choice of order and disorder in his or her working life. The inevitable disruption of the balance of order and disorder is the cause of stress to which the Lone Worker is particularly vulnerable.

The private life, what we shall later call 'support mechanisms', is particularly important for the survival of the Lone Worker because 'bad days' happen.

To work in total isolation can be most distressing and can cause additional pressure because it is through contact with others that the basic need for recognition is satisfied. Everyone has a fundamental need for recognition from others. At the very least you need others to recognise your presence and acknowledge you as a person, who you are and what you have done. The extent to which other people approve of you, the degree of liking they have for you, and the rewards you get for what you do are very important to your personal sense of well-being. As a Lone Worker the need for recognition is seldom fully met. Individuals can reduce the pressure of this unmet need by planning to meet this need elsewhere; or to re-evaluate your expectations to see whether they are appropriate.

In the allocation of time we need to arrange for human contact – not too little and not too much.

Dan is a writer. To live he needs to produce one book or 80 000 words and 20 articles of between 2000 and 3000 words per year. He works from home and lives two hours by train from his market – London publishers.

He has a family and his wife has a demanding job as a 'computer nursemaid' of a local insurance company. Working from home he has to handle the daily problems of real families – sick children, meter readers, door-to-door salespersons, washing machine repairs, etc. How does he organise his day?

The classical answer is discipline, but what does this mean?

Barbara has the example of those around her to impose the discipline. If she comes in late to work, people will notice. Her supervisor may well call her into his or her office and recriminations will begin, but the recriminations do not stop there. The others will *notice*. Barbara will have deviated from the workplace norm and it will be made obvious to her that it has been recorded – Barbara has overslept!

Alan and, much more significantly, Dan have no norms of discipline imposed on them from outside. If Alan oversleeps he can cover up and work quicker or later. If Dan, our writer, needs to collect children from school and take them to the doctors, he can work more intensively and *nobody* will ever know. Again there are limits.

Exercise 2.5

As a Lone Worker what latitude do you have in managing your day? What problems do you have in controlling the pressures against your effective management? How do you cope?

Somehow, all the time, the Lone Worker is faced with the statement 'It's your problem'. The need for human contact varies both in quality and quantity with individuals. Alan was very task-motivated but did not, as did Barbara, need to relate to the human race *en masse*. He did, however, have a significant need to relate to individuals.

When Alan structured his day he allowed for this human need: he would arrange to visit particular individuals with whom he related towards the close of the day so that he could 'stop and talk'. Motivated Lone Workers structure their time so that their basic needs for human contact are satisfied in the amount and quality they need to survive effectively.

Dan, our writer, has a very predictable and personal pattern for his working day. To write successfully he needs privacy and virtual seclusion which he finds in a small office at the top of his rambling home. The door to his office bolts and there is a large notice saying 'KEEP OUT'.

Dan begins his day by pottering and adjusting himself to his world. He has a very strict set of routines which finish with him playing computer chess on his word processor.

When he is 'good and ready' he gets down to write about 2000 words, either in primary form or in one of the numerous revisions that are his style. He then gets up and wanders to the local public house for his 'fix' of people. Once he feels that he has returned to the human race, he goes back to get something to eat, potters and starts work again for another 2000 words.

We would see five elements in the way we structure our time:

- The task itself with little or solely professional human contact.
- Private routines.
- People and noise *en masse*.
- Casual one-to-one contact.
- Serious and intimate one-to-one contact.

As we move down the five elements the quality of the human contact increases. Serious and intimate one-to-one contact has a great value on our imaginary scale whereas meeting people *en masse* in a busy public house has much less value but, on the other hand, is less risky to the individual.

Lone Workers with a great need for human contact may well structure their time towards the high value elements – people *en masse*, casual and intimate contacts. They may even find that their professional dedication to the task is confused with their need for human contact and that their personal routines somehow involve other people. Dan, our author, still needs his 'fix' but somehow obtains much of his 'ration' from casual one-to-one contact over a few beers.

We are suggesting that people set their 'human need ration' and meet it by balancing the five elements. If we find our needs are not being satisfied we can either increase the time we spend on one of the five elements or 'trade up' to a higher value element. We are also suggesting that we can have too much human contact for our own personal needs and need to 'trade down' our elements. Dan's family would be quite clear what that meant – he would quite suddenly withdraw from family contact and escape on a long walk by himself. We all need to determine our own balance of human contact, just as we need to determine our own balance of order and disorder.

One way of looking at personal stress is to see it as a disruption of one of the two fundamental life balances – human contact and order/disorder. The Lone Worker is particularly vulnerable because he or she has chosen to determine the balance themselves and not rely on others to do it for them.

Exercise 2.6

Let's take our two Lone Workers – Alan the insurance man and Dan our author. Using a pie chart technique, we have attempted to see how they distribute their time within the five elements:

- *The task itself with little or solely professional human contact.*
- *Private routines.*
- *People and noise en masse.*
- *Casual one-to-one contact.*
- *Serious and intimate one-to-one contact.*

Now you, the reader, use the remaining pie chart to analyse how you spend your time. Use the same categories as we have done for Alan and Dan.

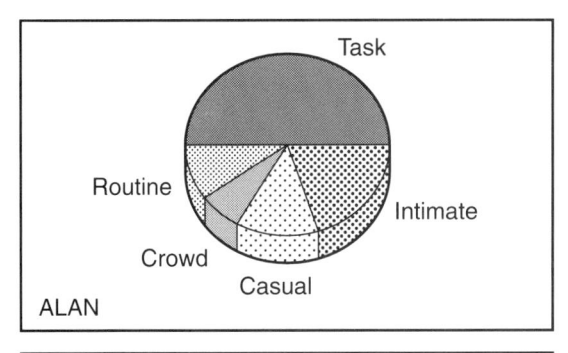

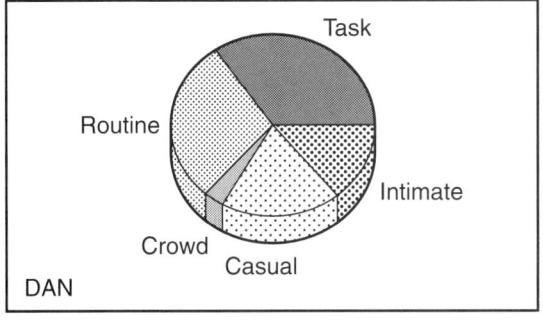

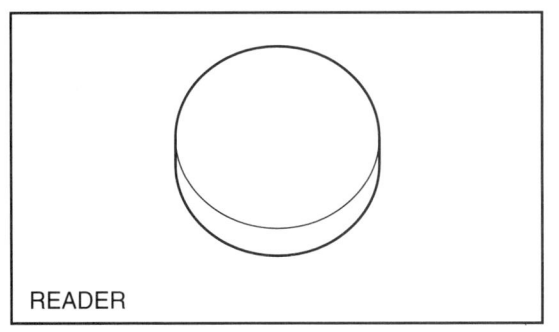

[Pie chart labeled ALAN with sections: Task, Routine, Crowd, Casual, Intimate]

[Pie chart labeled DAN with sections: Task, Routine, Crowd, Casual, Intimate]

[Blank pie chart labeled READER]

To continue to enjoy working under pressure, there are four main points to remember.

1. *Maintain the balance between your professional and private life.*

Few of us have complete control over our time. The way we divide up our hours inevitably depends upon the nature of our work and the structure of our personal life. The ideal balance of roughly eight hours spent at work and 16 hours of relaxing, eating and leisure activity can be hard to achieve. Under pressure we may lose sight of priorities and allow certain areas and activities to crowd out the others. The result is that life becomes increasingly stressful. Sleeping and eating are obviously vital functions to which we must devote sufficient time, but it is also important to learn how to waste time creatively. Having fun can prove therapeutic, because it increases your efficiency and contentment at work, as well as our capacity to unwind.

2. *Build up resources to remain in control.*
One of the signs of approaching strain is the sense of 'being out of control'. One can avoid such feelings by following simple guidelines.

- Plan your day: list your jobs and as you complete a job, strike it through and enjoy the satisfaction of completing the task.
- Give yourself rewards for success.
- Give yourself time to think and do not allow this time to be interrupted.
- Impose an order to your day and do not allow yourself to skip meals.
- Take time at the end of the day to review and prepare for the next day.

3. *Remember that you have the right to say 'NO' – it's your life anyway.*
Saying 'NO' is easier said than done. In Chapter 7 we will give some definitive advice.

4. *Plan your time but be aware of the needs of others.*
If you want to use your time more effectively, then you have to start by knowing how you are spending your day. Create a personal log.

Time of day	Activity	Interruption
7.00 am		
7.30 am		

Divide your day into 15-minute sections. Under the interruptions column indicate with a tick if you were interrupted and a cross if you were not.

Look at the activities and put them into some form of classification – meeting, travel, customer contact, sport/leisure, etc. Rate the activities in order of importance to your work and to your 'people needs'.

Once you have done this you are now in a position to take a time inventory of your life. Do this over a week and you will discover how you actually use your time and how you think you use it. The benefits of such an analysis are enormous. It is also useful to go through and mark those tasks which were profitable and those which were wasted.

Doing this will enable you to plan your daily schedule much more effectively at work, and balance this with home and recreational activities.

Support mechanisms

It is impossible for the balancing tricks we have discussed – that of order and disorder, obtaining the right amount of human contact and time management – to be perfect all the time. If we rely on work alone to establish the balance we will fail. We need to be able to take reserves from other 'accounts'. Our home and leisure lives need to act as a buffer against excessive demands or deficiencies in our work situation.

Fran is a window cleaner. Some years ago he had a reasonably sized business with several people working for and with him contract cleaning business premises. Fran is a very private man who has a very low need for the noise and bustle of the human race in general – a low (b) score for needing 'to belong' in our questionnaire in Chapter 1. The noise and bustle that goes with working in a team was compensated by his principal hobby – fishing. He was able to get away and, as he said, 'recharge his batteries'.

His business only just survived the recession, a survival made possible by his losing all his staff and working alone on the more profitable contract cleaning services.

Although he had a low need for human contact *en masse*, the new job left him feeling isolated and vulnerable. He did not drop his fishing but took up an additional hobby – following a local football club with a small group of friends. The new hobby, in a way that he can control, allows him to get sufficient 'belonging needs' to relax and overcome the stresses of working completely alone.

Our Lone Worker can withstand a certain amount of the stresses of imbalance but there are limits. Without support outside work the inevitable problems of stress will build up.

The exact role of the support mechanisms will be discussed in Chapter 8, but here it is sufficient to say that the world of work is remarkably unforgiving and that the stresses it produces can rarely be released without producing additional problems. Outside work it is possible to shout yourself hoarse at a sports meeting, as with Fran, or to take out your frustrations on a squash ball.

Real stress – real, dysfunctional stress – occurs when our support mechanisms fail.

3

Better safe than sorry – planning to avoid hazards

Legal responsibilities for safe working – Balancing risks and consequences – Establishing safe working procedures – The concepts of Diagnosis, Prognosis and Treatment Guidelines for safe working – Training and monitoring.

We discussed the many positive aspects of lone working in the first two chapters. From now on in the book we will consider many of the negatives and propose how these can be reduced, but not unfortunately, eliminated. Provided that the Lone Worker stays within his or her 'frame' the Lone Worker has many of the benefits of feeling self-employed and master of his or her own fate. However, organisations strongly discourage straying outside defined patches of personal responsibility. In the previous chapter we took the metaphor of 'bears and the squares' to develop the idea.

However, there are more dangerous 'bears' waiting for Lone Workers when they step on the lines, and these are the 'bears' that Diana Lamplugh discussed in her own book. The lines are guarded by the 'bears' who endanger the Lone Worker by threatening violence and abuse. Unfortunately the evidence is that the unofficial 'bears' are increasing in number. Life is not getting any easier for ordinary people doing their own appointed tasks.

It was estimated that in the month of October 1992 20 members of the Health Service and five post office workers – both men and women – were attacked by the people they are supposed to serve. It was also claimed that reported incidents were only the tip of the iceberg and that public service employees face almost daily verbal abuse, intimidation and harassment.

Everyone is at risk, but some professions render people more at risk than others.

Overall, we must not get the matter out of proportion. It has been estimated that there is one incident in about every 100 years of working life or, put the other way, in a 30-year working life we have a one in three chance of trouble. It is the reduction of the 'one in three chance during a working life' that every worker and employer has personal and professional responsibility to achieve. However, in our own work we have found that the risks concerned with 'accidents' to the Lone Worker must give greater concern than those due to physical or mental attacks by fellow man.

The purpose of this chapter is to discuss why we, both the employer and the employee, need to take safety seriously in all its aspects, and why we need to develop safe working procedures. Beyond the provisions of common law, there is the Health and Safety at Work Act and various Regulations based upon EC Directives, which came into force in January 1993 and are included in Appendix 5. We will begin with the legal aspect of responsibility for safe working as defined by the Health and Safety at Work Act, 1974.

Legal responsibilities for safe working

Putting things very simply, both employer and employed have a legal responsibility for safety at work. If an incident occurs, then there is a question of liability. Failure to comply to the Health and Safety at Work Act 1974 results in criminal sanctions. There is also a common law liability based on the tort of negligence.

> **Relevant sections from the UK Health and Safety at Work Act 1974.**
>
> *Duties of employers to their employees*
>
> 27 The general duty imposed on all employees is to ensure, so far as is reasonably practicable, the health, safety and welfare of all their employees. . . .
>
> 31 Employers must provide for all their employees the information, instruction, training and supervision, necessary to ensure, so far as is reasonably practicable, their health and safety at work . . . Employers must ensure that all their employees are competent to carry out their jobs in a safe manner, that is, with the minimum of risk to themselves or others. Section 2(2)(c)
>
> 47 As well as having responsibilities towards other people, the self-employed have a duty to carry on their businesses in such a way as to ensure, so far as is reasonably practicable, that they do not risk their own health and safety. Section 3(2)
>
> 66 All employees must take reasonable care for the health and safety of themselves and of other persons who may be affected by what they do, or fail to do, at work. This duty implies not only avoiding obviously silly or reckless behaviour, but also taking positive steps to understand the hazards in the workplace, to comply with safety rules and procedures and to ensure that nothing they do, or fail to do, puts themselves or others at risk. Section 7(a)

The Health and Safety at Work Act covers in detail accidents in the workplace. Such accidents could be injuries caused in the operation of a particular piece of equipment or could equally cover incidents of violence and abuse against the person. In both what we will term 'accidents' and 'incidents of violence or abuse', the Lone Worker is particularly at risk. A minor accident leading to injury untreated may lead to serious injury.

We were told of a man who, while working alone and about two miles from a telephone, fell and suffered a serious cut. Unable to summon help he crawled the two miles while attempting to reduce the bleeding with his thumb. Luckily, and through gross grit, he lived. Nobody was aware he was missing. He carried no alarm system or first aid kit.

In 'incidents of violence or abuse' the Lone Worker is doubly at risk because he or she is alone. The incidents are likely to be more frequent and the consequences are likely to be greater. The legal responsibility is real and an important reason for action, but there is perhaps a more pressing reason for taking increasing care – mutually enlightened self-interest. Many books have been written about the physical aspects of accidents at work and their avoidance. They are not the main subject of this book but cannot be dismissed in any book for Lone Workers and their managers.

Minor accidents can become serious if they are not treated competently and promptly and thus become an heightened risk for people who work without the support of colleagues.

Throughout our discussion we will see that the distinction between 'accidents' and 'incidents of violence or abuse' is vague. We make no apology for this, the consequences of either can be equally unpleasant. The individual victims and those around them stand to lose directly and indirectly from violence and abuse and so does their organisation. Violence in all its forms affects the organisation as a whole; frightened staff do not work to their full potential and incidents often mean lost time and sickness.

We were asked to advise a DHSS office – Direct Payments Section – on handling verbal abuse and threatening behaviour. The office was in a depressed urban area and the Direct Payments Section was regarded by the office as being the 'end of the line'. The women in the office handled telephone calls from members of the public in extreme distress:

'I have just been evicted and am on the pavement with my kids. I need help NOW.'

'I am 80 and the gas has been cut off – it's freezing in the flat. I need help NOW.'

The stories were all variations on the same theme but the approaches of the clients differed:

'I know you can get me the money, so **** get it. I know your name and where you live. If you don't get me the money just watch out for your *** kids . . .'

This last conversation went on for 15 minutes and at the end the whole office was exhausted. No further work was done during the day and the afternoon break did not confine itself to tea.

Abuse and violence, whether actual or threatened, costs real money, for example in time off, sickness pay, higher insurance premiums and even compensation payments. It is in everyone's interest to reduce incidents. However, security measures cost money, and although these costs can be measured the softer issues of benefits of improved morale and lower staff turnover are harder to quantify. There is therefore a very strong case for companies to employ effective methods of monitoring and assessing the methods they use to help reduce assaults.

If violence at work becomes a concern, employers should discuss drawing up a code of practice with their employees. The code should cover what is expected of staff if an attack takes place, what steps staff should take to protect themselves, and what support they can expect from the organisation in terms of time off and compensation, etc. By working together employers and employees can establish mutually acceptable and realistic, workable procedures for dealing with acts of violence. Such a code will be discussed below (*see* pages 40–57).

Establishing safe working procedures

Unfortunately many safety procedures come on the backs of 'incidents'. Someone is attacked before actions are taken – the stable door is locked after the horse has bolted. This need not always be so and the development of the Suzy Lamplugh Trust is a case in mind. Here one incident has been used to bring the whole subject of violence in the workplace to a general audience. The actions arising from such awareness may have prevented hundreds of similar incidents as people acknowledge the dangers to themselves or their staff and do something relevant about them. Relevance is the key. Adopting grandiose safety procedures without studying the actual work situation, without involving the workers who know, and without review and follow-up procedures is worse than useless. Talking to the people who know – the people who are actually involved – can also be very efficient.

WORKING ALONE

Diagnosis

Prognosis

Treatment

Health care

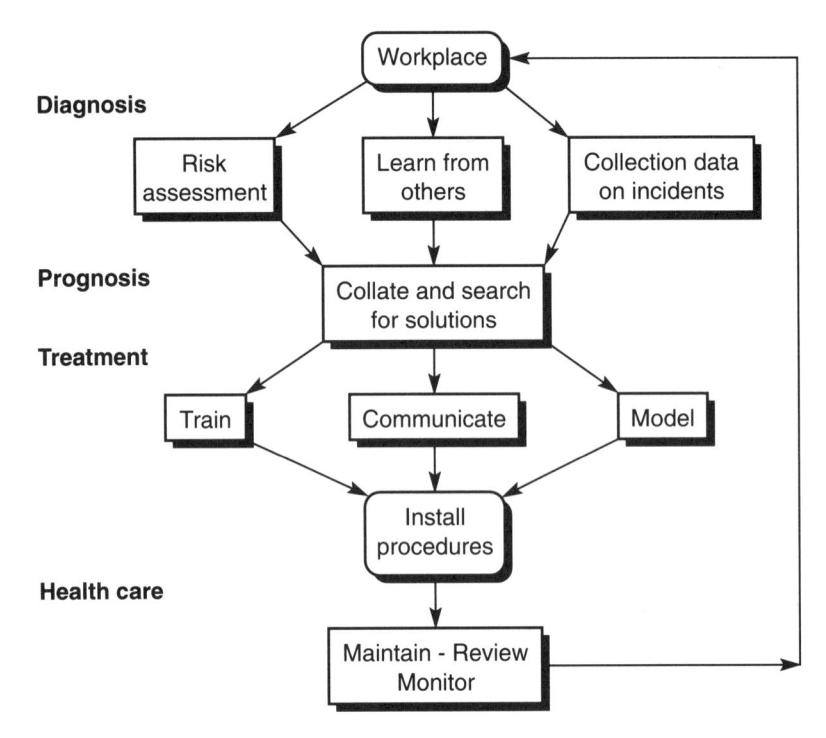

Figure 3.1 **Stages to establishing safe working procedures**

We discussed safety issues with a self-employed barber working in a lock-up premises at the end of quiet side street. His concern was being mugged by customers. In discussion we found that his customers were almost invariable respectable and many of them were children accompanied by parents. However, at the end of his day he always took his takings to the nightsafe of the local bank in a brief case. In the winter, this involved leaving his darkened shop and walking about 50 metres down the unlit side street.

The local police were very happy to arrange an informal escort at no cost. The precautions the barber was originally proposing would have incurred considerable inconvenience and cost.

There are four stages in establishing effective safe working procedures. We have called these diagnosis, prognosis and treatment and health care. They are summarised in Fig. 3.1.

Diagnosis: identifying potential risks

We have three diagnosis techniques, all of which can be used appropriately and independently. In each case the results need to be collated and stored systematically.

RISK ASSESSMENT: TALKING TO THE PEOPLE WHO KNOW

One way to investigate potential problems is to ask the people who know – the people at risk. Managers, trade union or health and safety representatives, or even external consultants, are probably in the best position to discuss matters informally or to conduct a survey. The whole process need only be applied to those areas of an organisation where there are employees who are in direct personal contact with the public. Risk assessment for companies with five or more employees needs to be formal, with an appointed manager for each area. The detailed approach is given in Appendix 5.

The results of the surveys or discussions should be reported back to staff for comment. The feedback not only ensures that the questioner has understood what has been said, but also affirms that problems, if they exist, are being acknowledged. Often we find that the problems are not what they seem and that discussion and feedback clarifies problems and allays fears. Other times we find that very simple precautions can reduce risks and lead to immediate and satisfactory measures being taken.

In the case of a formal risk assessment the forms need to be prepared and held by a nominated, appropriate and trained member of staff. Where the company is working with other companies, risk assessments and procedures may need to be exchanged.

LEARNING FROM OTHERS: WHO ELSE HAS THE PROBLEM?

An often disregarded diagnostic technique is 'learning from others'. Very few situations are unique and it is often possible to build on the experiences of others who operate in similar conditions. Just as Alan would discuss his round with other collectors, organisations can 'ask' other operators to check their plans.

Sophie Mirman, the founder of Sock Shop, extended her network of shops, successful in the United Kingdom, to New York. But her enterprise resulted in a disaster that could easily have been avoided with hindsight.

> We also thought that we could position the shops in high-pedestrian-flow areas in New York – in the subways, just as we had in London. We hadn't appreciated the violence and the number of drug-related attacks that go on in Manhattan. Junkies just walk in and attack the staff or hold them at gun point to steal from the till. We used to empty the tills very regularly, but they would still come in to steal a few dollars. We had to have armed security guards.

The problem virtually destroyed Sophie's empire but perhaps of more relevance to this book, gave several of her workers considerable personal problems. The whole tragedy might have been averted by 'asking' others who had operated in the same area.

INCIDENT RECORDING AND ANALYSIS

The third of the diagnostic techniques is perhaps the most obvious: using the accident reporting procedures already in place in the company. Most organisations have procedures for recording accidents and incidents but the systems vary. Managers can use standard accident report procedures and forms or, if they really want to learn from experience, use specially designed forms. We would recommend the latter system. An example is given in Appendix 1.

The ideal form should be designed for the clear purpose of providing sufficient help in establishing relevant safety procedures. An example of the use of such data came from Alan and Barbara's employers – the insurance company.

> The company collected data of incidents over several years and found a distinct pattern in the incidents, assaults becoming heavier at night and towards the weekends. With this information routes and schedules were

changed so that potential problem visits were taken mid-week, and during daylight hours in the winter. The conclusion is obvious, but by using the data, changes in practice became company policy and did not rely on the common sense of individual collectors.

Even with the present level of awareness, many assaults go unreported and the organisation and its employees may be lulled into a false sense of security. Various reasons for avoiding reporting assaults have been given, and certainly complex reporting forms feature on the list. In our view the forms should be as simple as possible, readily but discreetly available, and explained to all staff.

Sometimes it is the fear of being disciplined after an incident, accident or assault that prevents people from reporting such incidents. As a result, there is sometimes a tendency to avoid completing report forms or to 'economise on the truth' when completing them.

With an assault there is often the additional factor of a feeling of guilt, particularly in hindsight. The victims may feel that 'they did something stupid' or that they did not adhere to the letter of company procedures. Because of this reluctance it may often be necessary to assist people in the completion of the reports. For reports to be useful they need to be completed as soon after the incident as possible, *without* the 20:20 vision of hindsight.

It may be useful to remember that a brief description of the assailant may allow the organisation to identify particular sections of the public from which staff are most at risk. Allowing victims to give their impressions of the assailant and possible motives for the attack may identify weak spots in procedures which can then be tightened up. Provision for such impressions should therefore be included in the report forms. Fig. 3.2 shows the components of a good reporting procedure and the sorts of information to be acquired from report forms.

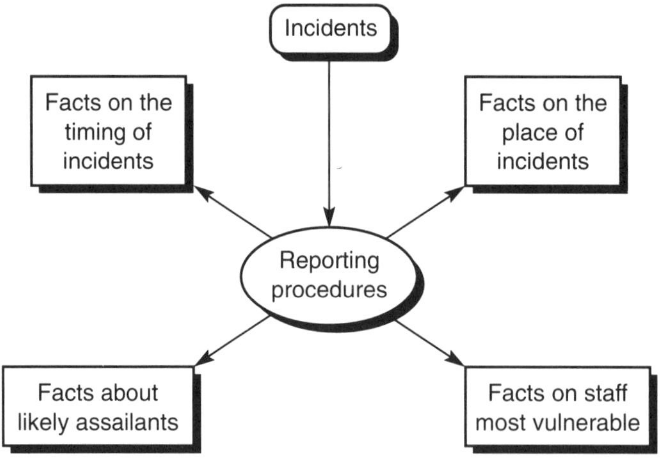

Figure 3.2 Reporting assaults

Prognosis: collation and classification of incident data

The information from the diagnostic stage needs to collected centrally, collated, acted upon, and be seen to be acted upon. The information from the three methodologies may well differ in formality and organisation and in this section we will be discussing primarily the information from the accident reports and the risk analysis.

Discussion with individuals and organisations working in similar areas may well lead to setting priorities – areas which merit attention. The risk analysis is likely to direct our efforts towards immediate actions – things that can and must be done with a minimum of delay. The incident record forms provide a basis for medium and long-term preventative measures but they should also be used as the basis of immediate action where this is called for. They must not be lost in a marsh of bureaucracy.

Ideally, the incident forms themselves should include sections to record follow-up actions taken, both in terms of preventative measures and of aftercare for the employees. Information on computer records should be limited because of the Data Protection Act 1984 under which those collecting information should be aware that the records are subject to 'Right of Inspection'.

In some areas of work, where the work involves repeated contact with individuals, the data from the reports may be collated into case files. These case files may well be used to:

- pre-warn new staff of potentially difficult clients; and
- prepare criminal or civil proceedings against individuals who assault or abuse staff.

The files should contain detailed information of any threatened or actual violent incident and a copy or reference to the violent incident report form should be available to any worker needing to work with the abusive, violent client in the future. Prepared with such information, special precautions can be taken in advance, for example visits might be made with a colleague, the time and place of the meeting can be adjusted, etc.

If the results from the reports show that there are only isolated incidents of violence which are quite different in kind, there is no case for initiating preventative action. If the data shows that some kinds of incidents are repeated then there is a case for further analysis. Whenever there are groups of similar incidents it should be possible to build up a picture of the type of incident and potential causes. Useful information can be gathered from these reports such as the type of assailant, the type of employee, the type of interaction between them and the situation in which the incident occurs.

The establishment of preventative procedures depends on understanding the risks involved. Very rarely do we have a 'new' situation and very often we can call upon others working in the same or similar area for assistance. Having said this, the data bank of actual incidents within an organisation can bring surprises.

An analysis of incidents in a riding school showed that virtually no problems were encountered between clients and staff and that physical accidents were both quite rare and never meant that injuries were left untreated over a significant period.

The problem that did cause the management and staff difficulties was that of obscene and abusive phone calls to the private lines of employees. These, treated professionally by experienced staff, were considered as 'part of the job'. However, they were a source of stress to younger workers. All that was needed was to allow the subject airing in the tack room. (*A British Telecom pamphlet is available on the handling of such calls.*)

Systematic analysis may well be of value in larger organisations to evolve a strategy of prevention.

THE ASSAILANT

The main factor that is likely to emerge from the analysis of assailants is their diversity. The warning is that it is *never* valid to make assumptions and accept stereotypes.

Talking to a trainee mental health nurse we were told of the first time he was seriously assaulted. He was doing his rounds with an experienced officer and checking whether everyone was prepared for the evening meal. There were various obviously distressed patients and one very quiet old lady just casting off her knitting in the corner. He turned his back on the 'sweet' old lady to deal with one of the distressed patents. The experienced officer only just prevented the old lady from inflicting permanent injury to him with the knitting needles.

It is also possible to give people due warning that you can or cannot do what they want.

An operator of a one-man newspaper stand was subject to repeated abuse and near assault. Discussion revealed that virtually all his 'assailants' were being refused change for the vending machines close to the stand. Although not preventing the problem, a notice clearly saying, 'No change given for vending machines' reduced the problem.

THE EMPLOYEE

The way jobs are designed can reduce the risk of violence. But there are no ready-made answers. Each individual has to find measures that are right for each workplace. In many jobs which are at risk from violence there is scope for intervention to enable the present and future workforce to cope more effectively. The very contentious issue concerned with the employee is that it may be supposed that certain classifications of employee are significantly more at risk than others: women more than men, young and aged more than a magic middle-aged group, coloured more than white, Catholic more than Protestant, etc. We will be discussing this issue, for which there are many prejudices but few analyses, in Chapter 9. The only point we would like to make here is that of common sense.

- If a job is truly dangerous for any sub-set of society, then perhaps it has to be treated differently and the precautions costed in at acceptance of the job.
- Just as certain jobs do require specific skills, certain jobs may require specific people. It is a positive and not a negative requirement.

An analysis of incidents may help us make decisions based on reason and not prejudice.

THE ENVIRONMENT OF INCIDENTS

Clusters of time and place may jump out from the analysis. The clusters, for example urban ghettos on weekends and in the evening, are unlikely to surprise the workers, but should help planning for safe practices.

A particular issue for postal staff is the delivery of unemployment giros in depressed areas. The staff know that they are subject to considerable abuse when the cheques are not on time for any of a myriad of different reasons, none of which are the responsibility of the delivery person. By collecting data the issue can be discussed and decisions made at a national level, should the problem increase.

Treatment: action to reduce incidents

The whole issue of analysis is to bring to formal notice the problems that can well be swallowed up in chatter. Lone Workers are unlikely to be the best communicators and their whole way of working precludes the informal reporting that can be used by their colleagues. Formal and centralised analysis should reduce the personal issues that surround virtually every individual incident and should allow strategic questions to be asked:

- Should we be doing this sort of work anyway?
- Can we change the job to give less face-to-face contact with the public?
- Are we asking too much of our staff?
- Have we got our costs wrong and should the job be done another way?
- Can we redesign the job so that our staff are no longer required to handle cash?

Several examples come to mind where analysis has led to direct action.

- Many insurance companies use direct debit to reduce the need for door-to-door collection.
- London Underground uses automatic ticket machines and automatic barriers to deal with the majority of transactions. The residual inspectors and collectors required to deal with marginal problems work in a small group.
- Many bus companies use cash machines and do not permit their staff to handle money in any way. They also reduce the need for money of any kind by adopting the practice used in mainland Europe for many years of buying multi-trip tickets from some central point.
- Toll collection points at bridges and tunnels have moved to cash collection bins and any movement out of the car or truck is not only obvious and recorded by visible cameras but also restricted by the design of the exit itself.

Any change is likely to be resisted unless those who have to work with it are committed. Simply being involved is not enough. Martina Navratilova defined the difference between involvement and commitment in terms of ham and eggs:

'The chicken is obviously involved but the pig is somewhat committed.'

Buses with a 'no change given' policy, cash bins at tolls, automatic ticket dispensers, etc., have all been opposed at their introduction. The only real way of getting involvement is by working with the people who are involved by using consultation, communication, training and monitoring.

Health care

Once the changes to reduce violence have been introduced, it is important to check how well they are working. Monitoring allows feedback from the operators, the elimination of less effective measures and the adoption of 'best practice', as it evolves, which can be spread throughout the organisation.

Best practice often leads to the development of a specific and accepted code of conduct for the whole organisation. At the end of the chapter we will quote extensively from one such code of practice developed for Skelmersdale Health Authority and look at the human resource management issues it raises. Before we do this we will discuss the wider consequences of introducing any change in work practice.

The guidelines for safe working

Any guidelines cannot be fully comprehensive because the range and extent of public contact is so extensive and the situations vary so widely. Each work situation or location may require different measures to prevent violence to staff. In companies which suffer an endemic problem with violence, there is a tendency for it to be accepted as 'part of the job', especially by those who do not suffer its effects directly. The number of violent assaults on staff has been growing throughout the 1980s. Companies which ten years ago experienced hardly any assaults on staff are now reporting increasing concern. However, we must make the assumption that any employee who deals with the public face- to- face is potentially at risk.

The most basic of all organisational changes is that of danger awareness and the most basic of rules to be enforced is that ALL employees must notify some central point of their movements. Even such a basic rule will bring resistance and will be opposed by those who see it as being an unnecessary restriction of freedom. Beyond the individual level, the culture of many organisations is about getting the task done at minimum cost; the whole concept of protecting the staff from risks, particularly in the controversial area of physical attack from customers and clients, is foreign. What very often happens is that lip service is paid until an actual incident takes place. The changes that are then made often have significance well beyond the obvious.

The Social Security measures introduced at the end of the Second World War were based on personal contact between the responsible officer and the 'client'. As the incidence of violence against officers increased many things changed, not least the physical layout of the DHSS offices themselves. Whereas in the old style offices the staff met their clients across a table, the new offices separated the workers from the clients by armoured glass panels. The new offices changed the motivational rewards of the offices. Before the changes many of the staff regarded working in the office and with clients as being a privilege and a relief from the tedium of paperwork but after the changes many saw it as the worst part of the job. Even the most friendly clients found themselves alienated and vented their anger in their relationships with the staff who had originally seen their job as being one of establishing empathy.

In the face of increasing concern it is not usually necessary to go beyond drawing up a code of practice, informing employees what is expected of them if an attack takes place, what steps they should take to protect themselves, and what support they can expect from the organisation in terms of time off, earnings protection and legal assistance. The code needs to be:

- universally understood, accepted and followed by all staff;
- tailored to the exact circumstances of the organisation and the individuals;
- reviewed regularly to maintain relevance; and
- enforced, monitored and modelled by all senior members of the organisation.

To make sure the code meets these four criteria, it should be developed in a consultative process – more about which will be included at the end of this chapter.

Typical code of conduct

AWAY FROM THE BASE AND IN THE COMMUNITY

- Wherever possible, in order that you can be traced as quickly as possible, you should inform someone, whether in the office, or, if you work alone, a neighbour or a friend, of where you are going and should always let people know about any alteration to your work schedule.

- It is advisable that you discuss with your management team any known history of violent incidents or circumstances which indicate that violent incidents might be anticipated, especially if you have an arrangement to meet or visit such a client. It is also important to remember that people are only human so that you should always tell your team information about any grudge held by a client against you. Wherever possible such information should be shared with colleagues as well as supervisors/managers.

This subject will be dealt with in more detail later under the heading 'REPORTING'.

- Care should always be taken when carrying a client in a car. Careful consideration should be given before doing this at all. If it is necessary to transport someone then:
    1. The client should sit in the rear seat.
    2. If the car has rear doors then childproof locks should be used where possible to provide further protection.
    3. If the client has a known history of violent incidents then an escort should sit in the back immediately behind the driver to minimise the risk of the client interfering with the control of the vehicle.

Various similar codes of practice arose from studies of violence to carers conducted by the then DHSS. The codes usually include recommendations that staff making visits outside the office should follow some simple, basic procedures to ensure their safety. We are quoting it in full as we expect that the concepts and principles can act as a template for other organisations.

The three guiding principles of the typical Code of Conduct are very much in the mould of the thinking we have already mentioned in the Introduction when we discussed the Lamplugh case:

- Let people know where you are going and when you expect to return.
- Learn from experience and pool that experience.
- Avoid wherever possible the identified major danger, for example taking a client in a car.
- Remember that there is the value statement – 'people are only human'.

CHECKLIST FOR EMPLOYEES WORKING AWAY FROM THE WORKSITE

Have you:
- ☐ a good understanding of the safety guidance procedures of your firm?
- ☐ a clear idea about the area into which you are going?
- ☐ carefully previewed today's visits? Are there any potentially violent cases?
- ☐ asked your manager to double up, take an escort or use a taxi if unsure?
- ☐ left your itinerary and expected departure/arrival times?
- ☐ told colleagues, manager etc. about possible changes of plan?
- ☐ arranged for contact if your return is overdue?

Do you carry:
- ☐ a personal alarm?
- ☐ a bag/briefcase or wear an outer uniform or have a car sticker that suggests you have money with you? Is this wise where you are going today/tonight?
- ☐ out-of-hours telephone numbers to summon help?

Remember
- ☐ to record any 'incidents' that occur using a violent incident report form (see 'REPORTING').
- ☐ the three 'Vs' of visiting: VET – VERIFY – VIGILANCE

CHECKLIST FOR MANAGERS

Are your employees who visit:
- ☐ trained in strategies for the prevention of violence?
- ☐ fully briefed about the area where they work?
- ☐ made aware of attitudes, trades or mannerisms which can annoy clients?
- ☐ given all available information about the client?

Have they:
- ☐ understood the importance of previewing cases?
- ☐ left an itinerary?
- ☐ made plans to keep in contact with colleagues?
- ☐ the means to contact you – even when the switchboard may not be in use?
- ☐ got your home telephone number or an alternative appropriate emergency number (and you theirs)?
- ☐ a sound understanding of the organisation's guidelines and procedures to assist in the management of aggressive behaviour?
- ☐ authority to arrange an accompanied visit, take an escort or use a taxi?

Do they:
- ☐ know where the violent incident report forms are located and are they familiar with them?
- ☐ know they have to record and report any 'incidents'?
- ☐ appreciate the need for procedure?
- ☐ know how to control and defuse potentially violent situations?
- ☐ appreciate their responsibilities for their own safety?

We make no apology for quoting in full from the DHSS Code of Practice. We only give one or two words of caution. The copy we borrowed contained various cynical comments including the following:

> ☐ asked your manager to double up, take an escort or use a taxi if unsure. *Fat chance!*

In the light of the cuts in social services expenditure the comments are probably valid but are a sore reflection on the failure to review the guidelines and maintain their relevance. If *any* guideline is seen to be 'cloud cuckoo', then the whole system will fall into disrepute.

Several issues emerge from the guidelines:

- the existence of a database of 'difficult' clients/situations;
- consultation and relevance;
- safety equipment and its availability;
- the importance of training; and
- commitment from the top down.

THE EXISTENCE OF A DATABASE

The existence of a database of 'difficult' clients and/or situations from which employees can learn from others' experiences is a primary, but often missed, opportunity for protecting staff.

CONSULTATION AND RELEVANCE

Some time ago we were called upon to plan a training programme for a very large organisation employing a range of people as Lone Workers. Our training programme was designed to provide a sophisticated answer to the human communications issues raised by the guidelines. The Lone Workers enlisted for our pilot training worked in a range of hazardous situations where physical danger was obvious and basic precautions were absent. The training programme collapsed and the company set about reviewing its entire procedures. The provision of basic safety equipment was the overall priority.

The consultation process can also avoid the 'fat chance!' syndrome. If 'management' actually believes that double manning is a possibility and the people on the ground know it has no chance of reality, then there is a fundamental discrepancy in thought here. For example, if there was an incident regarding the double-manning procedures of an organisation and the case was taken to a court of law, the discrepancies of thought would emerge and make the company look very foolish, and somebody may have been injured unnecessarily. *Consultation* is the key to providing *relevant* route to safety for all workers and in particular for Lone Workers. The sophisticated techniques that feature in this book will deal with a minority of incidents, but consultation is the key to dealing with the majority.

SAFETY EQUIPMENT AND ITS AVAILABILITY

Safety in all its aspects has to be a way of life. Unless senior management models the concept of safety and shows that it is concerned about safety procedures, it is a waste of time.

We were working with a civil engineering contractor and visiting a site that was under pressure. The regional manager was not expected. As we drove on site the agent conspicuously dashed up a ladder and explained in very basic English that what was being done by the workmen was unsafe. It was only on his way down that he put on his *own* safety helmet!

The obvious message that goes round the organisation is that 'when you are senior management you do not need to wear the safety footwear, safety helmets, etc., The actual message that is understood by everyone working within the organisation is that 'to become senior management it is necessary not to care about wearing safety boots, helmets, etc.'

So what is the basic safety equipment for the Lone Worker? Well, of course it depends on the job and that needs consultation. One large and diverse organisation we have worked with decided to standardise a particular form of safety boot. They were good boots with steel toe caps. Unfortunately half the workers had minimal problems with falling weights but were vitally concerned with slipping on muddy terrain. The 'good boots' had no heavy treads and were actually dangerous for these people. If the workers had been consulted, then maybe the error would never have been made.

Safety equipment is doubly important for the Lone Worker because it does not simply provide 'First Aid'. For the Lone Workers, what may be a simple accident to others, can become a major accident for them as they cannot rely on 'community support' within minutes. Like the man mentioned earlier who had an accident two miles from the nearest telephone, he nearly bled to death while trying to reach assistance.

Regarding safety, therefore, there are two basic rules for Lone Workers:

1. any necessity for safety equipment is doubly important for the Lone Worker; and
2. the basic issue is getting assistance as soon as possible.

Of course, technology has provided an answer in portable telephones, but even here there are drawbacks: will the phone be available when it is needed?

We have examples of car 'phones that were a considerable distance from Lone Workers when they needed them. We also have examples of car 'phones being connected to switch boards that 'went home' out of office hours and of other switch boards that were totally incompetent in rallying assistance. If, as managers of Lone Workers, you consider equipping your 'staff with portable telephones or car 'phones, look and monitor the *whole* system. Treat any emergency system as you would a fire alarm – test it regularly.

Personal alarms and other deterrents are also a good idea but they too need to be tested.

Postal delivery workers were given 'dog repellents' to test. The repellent emitted an ultrasonic scream that in test conditions paralysed dogs – the major cause of accidents to delivery staff. In practice the alarms took so long to take out of the all weather gear the delivery staff had to use that the dogs got a bite before they got an earful!

Again, the importance of consultation with staff using the equipment and understanding the job in its full reality are apparent.

THE IMPORTANCE OF TRAINING

Consultation is only the beginning. The decisions which result need to be communicated. On the most basic level First Aid and Fire drill procedures need to be taught. On a much more serious level it is not enough to make recommendations hoping that they will satisfy the law and the situation. Employees need to have:

- a sound understanding of the organisation's guidelines and procedures in dealing with potentially aggressive situations;
- training in strategies for the prevention of violence;
- been made aware of attitudes, trades or mannerisms which can annoy clients; and
- knowledge on how to control and defuse potentially violent situations.

These are not standard skills that come with the school leaver or the graduate. These are skills that are difficult to acquire and involve application. They are the subject of what is virtually the rest of this book.

COMMITMENT FROM THE TOP DOWN

If the management of any organisation chooses to see safety as an issue of the 'shop floor' then anything we are about to say is wasted. It is imperative that safety guidelines and procedures are seen to affect EVERYBODY in an organisation and that senior managers are seen to encourage and enforce codes of conduct.

In the next chapter we will begin to look at the interaction between Lone Worker, the job and the 'client' and develop a systematic way of planning for safer working.

4

Nobody wants dead heroes

*Eileen and the angry farmer – Agreeing on objectives –
Different roles need different tactics – Setting objectives –
Personal maintenance.*

Factors that, in hindsight, may have contributed to the Suzy Lamplugh disappearance were a lack of adherence to safety procedures, the possible ambiguity of her objectives and a very possible refusal to recognise obvious danger signals. In the last chapter we discussed safety procedures and came to the conclusion that systems:

- not universally observed were worse than useless;
- must be tailored to the exact circumstances of the job and be reviewed regularly;
- must be followed by ALL staff; and
- must be enforced, monitored and modelled by the senior members of the organisation.

In this chapter we will develop the problem of ambiguity of objectives and set out a way that the reader can look at his or her job more clearly.

We are looking toward professionalism as a way of improving both safety and job satisfaction.

Eileen and the angry farmer

Very early in our work with Lone Workers we were presented with a case where a pollution control officer had been shot at by an irate farmer. The officer was asking for sympathy and advice on how she should deal with similarly irate people in the future. Eileen's story was this.

There had been a report of pollution in the river passing through the farmer's land and Eileen, as the officer responsible, had decided to investigate.

The procedures discussed in the previous chapter had been followed: the visit had been logged, gloves were worn, the Land Rover was correctly serviced and parked for easy departure, etc. Eileen was working with her sampling bottles in a ditch partially obscured by a hedge when the farmer arrived. The farmer made some violent comments about it being his land. Eileen dropped her sample bottles and ran towards the gate and her Land Rover. It was at this point that the farmer fired and, luckily, missed.

We never met the farmer but asked Eileen to put herself in his shoes. What did the farmer see, hear and feel about the incident? Eileen, putting herself in the farmer's role, remembered that there had been a hippy invasion in the district the previous week and that there had been considerable confusion and some damage and violence. She could well have been, in the farmer's mind, the vanguard of a further hippy convoy to desecrate *his* land this time. With this background Eileen was able to picture the scene through the farmer's eyes: there was this stranger, wearing a slightly battered Barbour jacket, crouching in his ditch.

Looking at it from the farmer's point of view Eileen was able to sympathise. She even thought that a shot intended to speed her on her way was probably quite understandable, if not actually justified. The obvious question came up in the subsequent discussion: how was the farmer supposed to know who Eileen was and that her presence on his land was perfectly legal? Eileen had given him no prior warning of her arrival – there had been no telephone call or letter of notification. She was wearing a uniform of sorts – ageing waxed jackets seemed to be the accepted 'uniform' of all the officers in her group, but the farmer was hardly likely to know this. To the farmer, Eileen was not a representative of authority – she was a trespassing stranger. Obviously, if challenged in a less aggressive way she could have presented identification and legally what she was doing was correct. The fact was that her behaviour had produced a violent reaction that could well have led to physical injury.

From the farmer's stand-point, therefore, he did not know the 'stranger's' reason for being on *his* land. From Eileen's stand-point there is a more serious problem: Eileen did not have a single, clear purpose for her being on his land.

Agreeing on objectives

Eileen's organisation had as its expressed objective the promise of cleaner rivers throughout its working area. Eileen understood this objective when she joined and was very happy to be associated with it – the objective fitted into her own values and beliefs. When we asked her how she would like to be spoken of when she retired she told us that she would like to be remembered as having made a positive contribution to making and enabling fish to swim in all the areas for which she had responsibility.

Exercise 4.1

- *What is the purpose of your organisation? This may or may not be formalised into a mission statement.*
- *Now imagine you are about to retire and a colleague is presenting you with a memento for your period of service with the organisation. How is the colleague describing your achievements?*

If you are lucky, then your own personal vision will fit the organisation's purpose. What it will not say is how you achieve your vision. (We will discuss the problems when there is a mis-match later in the chapter.)

Agreeing on general purpose is a good beginning: 'If we do not know where we are going, we will certainly arrive somewhere else'. However, agreeing on a destination does not settle how we intend to get there – what our tactics are.

Tactics determine our behaviour.

In discussing her job Eileen explained her tactics. She saw it as necessary to 'catch' polluters by collecting sufficient evidence to enable her to prosecute if necessary. Hopefully, she continued, such strong-arm behaviour was not often necessary, and she would like to achieve her purpose by providing advice for avoiding future pollution.

On the face of it, Eileen's objectives are quite clear but in practice she is giving herself three quite distinct roles:

- as a detective collecting evidence against polluters;
- as an adviser who provides sensible advice to help legitimate business people continue their business with minimum pollution; and
- as a law enforcement officer issuing a range of penalties ranging from a strong telling off to an enforcement order.

Unfortunately, each of the roles demanded a quite different approach: a person acting in the detective role uses stealth whereas the adviser acts as a knowledgeable and available friend and someone acting in the enforcement role uses firm authority.

Eileen had all three roles in her mind when she went to see the farmer. She was first acting as a detective attempting to 'catch him out'. Once 'caught out', Eileen 'the enforcer' had hard evidence to act as a starting point for some stricture which she saw as a method of preventing further pollution. At any point she was happy to switch into Eileen 'the adviser' provided 'he behaved reasonably'. No doubt the progression of roles was clear to Eileen but we suspect it was virtually impossible to convey to the farmer. He had at best caught a snooper acting in an undignified way. One does not take advice from snoopers let alone accept admonitions!

The three overall purposes of Eileen's job demanded different behaviour and with such a confusion of purpose in Eileen's mind, there was no possibility of the farmer understanding clearly what she was doing on his land.

Ambiguity is the greatest source of conflict. People like to know with whom they are dealing.

Exercise 4.2

Take one situation where you have found it difficult to relate to a client, customer or member of the public. What was your objective in the contact? Look with care at the objective and list the roles that you might perceive for yourself and the roles that might be presumed by the 'contact'.

Only when we have decided what our objective *is* can we decide how to achieve it. Thinking hard about the position Eileen found herself in, we find that her three roles demanded incompatible forms of action (*see* Table 4.1).

Table 4.1 The conflict of roles

	Detective	Adviser	Enforcer
Dress	Plain clothes	Appropriate clothing	Uniform
Bearing	Invisibility – stealth	High profile – recognised by sight	Distancing
Immediate behaviour	Questioning others and taking evidence	Access to experts – respect	Strong-arm support
Long-term plan	Irregular visits	Regular visits – surgeries – accessibilty	Planned interventions
Method of communication	—	Articles in local papers – newsletter	Clear and inflexible rules and procedures to follow
Relationship	Suspicion – potential enemies	Friend	Representative of higher authority

The three purposes demand different relationships and different behaviour. Unless Eileen is clear on her objectives and her role, and thus her relationships and behaviour, she will be confused. Confusion breeds conflict and can therefore be dangerous; you may be able to work with the ambiguity, but others may not be so gifted. Thus:

The Lone Worker needs to be very clear as to his or her purpose in every contact with 'clients'. Once the purpose is understood the relationship between the Lone Worker and the client can be considered and alternative forms of behaviour developed.

Exercise 4.3

Choose one from the list of Lone Workers below and list the alternative roles that might be seen to exist between the Lone Worker and his or her 'clients'. Search out the potential conflicts in behaviour that playing more than one of the roles simultaneously might bring.

Taxi drivers *Railway guards*
Teachers and trainers *Bar staff*
Policemen and women *Night sisters*
Postal delivery workers *Social workers*
Journalists *Your own example*

Once we have decided the overall purpose of the job we need to look at the way in which the purpose can be achieved and what role we need to play to achieve it.

Different roles need different tactics

The situation of Eileen and the angry farmer is that the farmer is being accused of being the likely source of a significant river pollution. Eileen decided initially that her purpose (i.e. pollution reduction) could best be achieved by collecting enough data for her to either act as an 'enforcer' or an 'adviser'. She wanted to be on solid ground whatever happened. Her initial role was therefore that of a 'detective'.

We would say that the detective role is probably the one of highest risk and certainly would involve very careful planning – there must be no short cutting in the application of safety procedures. Before setting out on her detective role Eileen would hopefully decide what she was looking for and what her course of action should be if she found it.

The details of her plans are not relevant but what is relevant is the sort of thing that she might find:

- Some signs of pollution which may or may not be clearly related to a direct flouting of the law.
- Some previously undiscovered source of pollution outside the responsibility of the farmer.
- Conclusive evidence of deliberate flouting of the law.
- Signs of ignorance or lack of maintenance.

The first two outcomes will call for further work in her detective role, the third – that of conclusive evidence – calls for the enforcement role and the last for some form of advisory role. She might have chosen the advisory role first in which case the signs she would have monitored would be the response of the farmer. She might then have had to switch into one of the alternative roles.

The point is that each of the roles calls for different behaviour and if you confuse the roles then it is likely you will confuse the behaviour. Confused behaviour can well lead to problem situations.

Tactics are all very well but they do not always work. The key is being able to change tactics when they are beginning not to work. Lone Workers need to know when to change tack. They need to know when they are not getting across and have alternative behaviours available. When Eileen found that the farmer was getting angry and threatening to shoot at her she needed to recognise that her 'detective role' was not working and that she needed to change her role. When Alan found that the pensioner had died he was able to change from a bustling attitude to one of care and consideration.

Setting objectives

A particular issue that needs to be emphasised is the setting of objectives – these *must* be what we have called *'professional'*. Looking at perhaps the biggest group of Lone Workers, those engaged in the caring professions, we see the greatest problems of ambiguity. Often the purpose of the job does not meet the vision of those filling the job.

Frank is a mental nurse working with acutely disturbed and often violent patients. For various reasons the budgets of the local authority in which he works have been cut drastically. The group Frank joined had a purpose of rehabilitation and the role Frank most enjoyed was that of a small group counsellor.

After the cuts and with the reduction in staff, small group work became impossible and his job became a 'damage limitation' exercise. Frank's purpose became one of providing a decent level of care. His role had ceased to be one of counsellor and had become much more routine. By continuing to see himself in the 'counsellor role', but with insufficient resources, he is bound to fail and offer things that he cannot provide to all those who demand it. The ambiguity of his position could well open him up to abuse if not real danger.

The problem of such ambiguity in the case study is very common – particularly in times of tightening budget constraints. The jobs people 'signed on for' and found rewarding are gradually altered – the lines between our squares move – and either we do not understand what has happened or, in many cases, refuse to accept the change.

Harry was a mental nurse working in a day-care centre. The centre was set up to relieve the pressure on carers who looked after highly disturbed dependants. In the days of easy funding carers would leave the dependant for negotiated periods knowing that they would receive professional caring help and that they could themselves have 'time out'. Harry particularly liked being able to discuss and advise the carers when they collected their charges.

As financial constraints were imposed on the unit Harry was asked to take increasing numbers of 'permanent' clients from other parts of the Health Authority and the space for the stop-over dependants decreased alarmingly.

Harry was particularly friendly with one carer who had two disturbed teenagers, one of whom was catered for by the centre. On a home visit the carer – the disturbed boy's mother – asked him to take the second teenager. Harry agreed informally but later had to tell the mother that he was unable to fulfil his promise. The mother got very abusive indeed.

What has happened is that Harry has moved into what we can call 'role confusion'. To the mother he has always been seen in the role of a family friend who *can* and *does* help professionally. This is the Harry that has come into her home before and she recognises. When Harry takes on the role of what she sees as a skinflint – the custodian of the public purse role – she meets a stranger. Harry's own genuine confusion and apology for having to take on such a role only makes matters worse.

Exercise 4.4

Think of the objectives you have in your job. List what you see as the objectives of your organisation now, and if you have been in the job for over five years, list the objectives of five years ago.

Is there any movement of objectives in your job over the five-year period and, if this movement occurs, how does it fit your own objectives now? If such a discrepancy exists, under what circumstances could it lead to role confusion?

Thus, from a Lone Worker's point of view, it is important to have fixed objectives and to monitor these objectives. Outside factors often impinge on a work situation and in doing so can lead to a change of objectives. Lone Workers should be aware of such changes and be prepared to set new objectives. In this way they can avoid the discrepancies that can result in role confusion which can, in turn, lead to dangerous situations.

Personal maintenance

The final step in our progress is to achieve what we have called 'personal maintenance'. Our point here is that when we work in a team and with colleagues there is very often someone who makes the tea, pours out the coffee, or simply decides that 'enough is enough'. The team often has devices to celebrate its successes and relieve the tensions of its failures. These diversions are an essential part of all work and can be almost assumed in teams, but have to be provided by the Lone Worker him or herself. Without them tensions will build up, as will real dysfunctional stress.

Eileen, when she was forced by circumstances to act in the enforcement role – a role she found personally stressful – would provide for her own personal maintenance. She would give herself time to relax. She would reward herself with some little treat which would often come in the form of a very indulgent cream cake. In the case of our insurance agent, Alan, you may remember that he used to arrange for space to have a drink with a friend after situations he found stressful. Both Alan and Eileen had learnt that Lone Workers have to look after themselves in all respects.

'Incidents' take it out of you. Stress is real and it kills. The body, accustomed to 'civilised' behaviour, sets about preparing to defend itself when it is attacked – it prepares to fight or run. The civilised man is not usually able to do either but the body does not know that. Our pulse races but we attempt to remain calm.

Ian is a door-to-door salesman. On this occasion he was selling encyclopedias in a council estate to a woman with several children. The conversation was going well and he was pretty certain of a sale. After about 20 minutes into his pitch the woman's partner arrived.

The partner was 'very unhappy' to find another man in the house and on being told that the other man was not a lover but a salesman for encyclopedias was far from reassured. Ian employed a cocktail of the techniques (that we will introduce in the next chapters) and avoided the very obvious physical violence offered him.

Ian got out, after about ten minutes, with his samples and his body undamaged. He went back to his car and panted for about 20 minutes. He then drove to the nearest café where the waitress, a relative stranger, sat him down and fed him a coffee. It was about half an hour later before his pulse rate was down to normal.

Ian was lucky to find a sympathetic waitress. When we find ourselves having to manage a difficult situation we need to maintain ourselves and allow our bodies to come back to normal. With no team or colleagues to rely on, Lone Workers must learn to account for their own personal maintenance.

In the next chapter we will look further at recognising the signals that give us advance warning of problems. We will see how certain situations can change from the essentially safe to the potentially dangerous. We will use the metaphor of traffic lights and spend time in looking at how we can tell when 'the lights are about to change from green to red'. When they are on amber is the time to worry.

5

Points of Risk

What is aggression? – Physical and verbal aggression – the incidence of incidents – Hazardous things, hazardous people – The principle of the 'traffic lights' – red, amber and green – What makes the lights change?

What is aggression?

As with much of 'people theory', there is a divided camp. The camp is divided into three main schools, dominated by concepts of basic biology, psychology and sociology. Again as with much 'people' theory, particular schools are most suited for dealing with particular situations and the truth lies in some sort of mixture with a probable new ingredient still to be discovered.

In looking at mankind, certainly the most complex mechanism in our perceived world, we do not expect a simple picture. Imagine attempting to describe a quite elementary machine from drawings taken from one position – say the side aspect only. It would be ridiculous. Man is no elementary machine and we need to describe and discuss him from many aspects.

The **biological school** lays the blame for aggressive behaviour on our genetic constitution and members of the school would maintain that we inherit our aggression from our ancestors through our genes. They would see hormones, and in particular the male sex hormone, as being largely responsible for the release of our inherent aggression. By linking aggression to our genetic make-up the biological school of thinkers imply that aggressive behaviour cannot significantly be moderated by any psychological or social intervention. For the Lone Worker the only protection would be a database built up by sad experience.

The **psychological school** suggests that aggression is a basic inborn force or drive which is present within all of us. The inborn force constantly generates hostile impulses which need to be continuously released. Members of the school see aggression as natural and as powerful as sex and point to the behaviour of young children who are more than willing to show aggression when things do not go their way. However, as children grow older they learn, hopefully, that they do not always get what they want by being aggressive. They learn to moderate their hostile instincts.

Golding, in his book the '*Lord of the Flies*', develops the concept of the innate aggression of children where apparently 'civilised' children in savage conditions revert to savagery.

Learning that aggressive responses are not always appropriate would seem the subject of education and socialisation but the Lone Worker needs to remember that it does not always happen. In many societies aggression appears to be successful and may be even actively encouraged (for example, the 'He who Dares Wins' philosophy). The aggressive individual does not need to develop alternative responses. In the psychological school it is maintained that aggressive display, even if modified by circumstances, still needs to be released, but the release is under socially acceptable conditions – for example, on a football pitch or squash court.

The **sociological school** emphasises the environmental context within which aggression and violence occur. Members of the school tend to see it as a rational response to the structure and functioning of society.

For the Lone Worker the issues of both the psychological and sociological schools are probably the same – there is more risk of violence in 'problem' areas. The biological school simply indicates that there are 'problem' people. The political and penal aspects of the three schools has aroused at least as much debate as the intellectual argument. For the Lone Worker faced with a 'problem' person, the intellectual debate may well seem academic. Our definition of aggression is therefore about results and not about intent or motive.

Aggression is a form of behaviour involving intent to hurt, either physically or emotionally, another human being.

What then is the definition of violence? The Health and Safety Executive's working definition of violence is:

Any incident in which an employee is abused, threatened or assaulted by a member of the public in circumstances arising out of the course of his or her employment.

Verbal abuse and threats, the Health and Safety Executive notes, are the most common types of incident. Physical assaults, both casual and premeditated, are comparatively rare. The HSE explains that *casual assaults* can stem from any number of motives, including alcohol and frustration. In the casual attack something is probably necessary to trigger the attack and the Lone Worker, or indeed any worker can, with skill, reduce the risk by allowing the potential attacker to save face, by making concessions, by empathising with them, or by simply listening and responding.

Verbal abuse is a threat which is more difficult to define in terms of the effect it has upon the victim. The problem for the Lone Worker is that it is difficult sometimes to remain cool and unprovoked if abused verbally. One thing may lead to another. There is also a thin dividing line between 'justifiable comment' and abuse, and for that reason many organisations only record incidents where actual physical injury has resulted. However, the example of the effect of verbal abuse in the DHSS office, that was discussed in Chapter 3, was real. The Courts are also beginning to recognise psychological damage as an entity. The concept of 'show us your wounds first' is fading. Proof of intent as opposed to concrete evidence is becoming accepted.

The situations which give rise to verbal abuse are often identical to those where an actual assault occurs, and a careful analysis of 'near misses' can have implications for the prevention of violence. The mood is changing and it is becoming accepted that there is a continuum of violence running from verbal abuse to physical attack, and the two should not be arbitrarily separated. Actual data, as we explained before, is difficult to obtain and may well not show the correct picture. Figures for the number of assaults on staff by the public are not separately identified on official crime statistics. However, according to research by the Labour Research Department in 1987, heavily slanted towards local authorities, 98 per cent of workplaces had experienced instances of abuse or harassment. Threats of violence had been made in 85 per cent of workplaces. Actual violence had occurred in 62 per cent of workplaces, including 80 per cent of transport companies and 77 per cent of health authorities. In 28 per cent of workplaces, there was experience of violence involving a weapon.

Other research, carried out by the Suzy Lamplugh Trust, showed that 8.1 per cent of respondents had encountered a physical attack in their current job, and 19.6 per cent had been subjected to threatening behaviour. The figures differed according to sex: physical attacks were reported by 11.6 per cent of men, compared to 7.3 per cent of women; threatening behaviour had been experienced by 24.6 per cent of men and 18.3 per cent of women, but again we must question the accuracy of reporting. A recent case in America has shown that *one* outspoken woman can encourage many less assertive fellows to report what they have previously withheld privately out of shame or fear for their jobs.

The highest levels of attack and abuse in this survey were reported by professional staff working outside the office. Particularly at risk were carers and retail staff in general. The British Crime Survey for 1988 showed that a quarter of crime victims said that the incident had happened at, or because of, work. (These incidents need not have necessarily involved a member of the public.) In the same survey 14 per cent said that they had been verbally abused at work at least once in the previous year. A third of all threats of violence were received at work.

The figures, such as they are, suggest a real problem and one that both workers, employers and society at large needs to concern itself with. It is a real problem and everything we have heard, read and experienced suggests that the problem is growing.

Again, we are discussing the outcome and not the cause or concepts – if someone has been assaulted, that is enough. The motivation of the aggressor in an assault is for the courts to decide, but the injury, mental or physical, remains whatever the courts decide. A basic strategy for Lone Workers is to be *forewarned is to be forearmed*. Cowards die many times before their deaths, but we are not asking Lone Workers to be fearful of every bush. Nevertheless, the price of survival is eternal watchfulness. Sometimes the price can be too high.

Hazardous things, hazardous people

Certain things are intrinsically dangerous. A sharp knife is an actual hazard to a child, or indeed, any unskilled user. In the hands of an experienced fishmonger, the knife is still a potential hazard but because he or she is used to working with sharp knives and takes relevant precautions, it is much less likely to cause unscheduled damage.

As it is with things, so it is with situations. Certain situations are *intrinsically* dangerous[1] – working from an unguarded ladder or dealing with violent people. These things and situations are obviously hazardous and because they are so obviously hazardous, only the foolhardy will not take precautions.

---

[1] We mentioned in the Introduction the intrinsic danger in certain situations makes them unsuitable for lone working, for example high-voltage electricity, rapid-moving machinery, rowing boats, dangerous chemicals, etc. In our experience the wise guidelines suggesting that such obviously dangerous situations do not permit lone working are sometimes ignored, and we would like the guidelines enforced. Here, however, we are discussing areas of less obvious intrinsic danger.

This can also be said of many sports such as caving, hang-gliding, rock climbing. The very obvious hazards they present means that those undertaking them are likely to take relevant precautions and training.

Many everyday activities are also intrinsically dangerous – driving cars, crossing the road, flying with a scheduled airline – but *because* it is usual to take precautions, the dangers, although still present, are much reduced.

There is an old story about a parish councillor who was advised to erect a sign in a local beauty spot much used by courting couples. The sign said 'KEEP OFF, DANGEROUS CLIFF'. After several years with no accidents the sign was removed on the basis that since nobody had fallen off recently, the cliff was no longer dangerous.

Certain things or activities although not intrinsically dangerous in themselves are in certain specific situations, dangerous. A example would be friendly family pet dog who becomes vicious when she feels her pups are being threatened.

For the Lone Worker a short cut down a back street may be perfectly reasonable in broad daylight, but is asking for trouble on a dark night. The postal delivery worker may find that steep stone steps may become dangerous in icy conditions. Each one of us weighs the risk against a certain internal scale: '*Am I willing to accept this level of risk?*' The question may even become more sophisticated: '*Am I, or the organisation I work for, willing to take the precautions necessary to reduce the risk to a level of personal acceptability?*' If the answer to the question is NO, then the Lone Worker must be ready to accept the consequences.

In a film sponsored by the Suzy Lamplugh Trust a female insurance salesperson explains a hazard that she felt unable to accept, however well she planned. The area she was expected to visit was a run-down council estate where law and order, in her opinion, had failed. For her, the intrinsic dangers remained unacceptable.

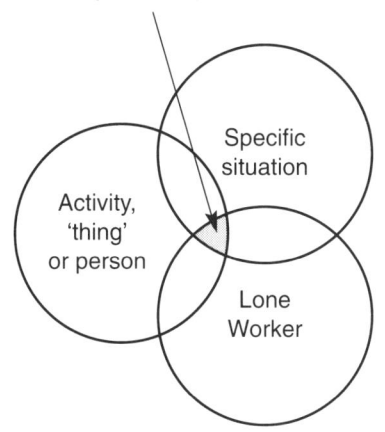

Figure 5.1 Interaction of the Lone Worker, a specific situation and intrinsic dangers

What we are considering here is an interaction between the Lone Worker, the intrinsic dangers of the 'thing' and the very specific situation (*see* Fig 5.1). The lone female worker visiting a dangerous area at night may well present what any prudent adult would consider as an unacceptable risk. The prudent adult will then think of the consequences: '*In my view the organisation may well accept my decision officially but I may well lose my job*'.

The female insurance agent above may find her actions supported along the official line, but in real terms could be singled out for unfavourable treatment at the first opportunity. In practice, and certainly in the past, the threat of the organisation taking on a worker who will accept risks that a prudent person will refuse, has caused some normally prudent people to act outside their personal zone of comfort, to drive them into stressful and dangerous situations where the price of vigilance is too high.

We were working with a group of Lone Workers identifying areas of risk and concern. There was a formal procedure for logging out before a job that was considered intrinsically dangerous by individual Lone Workers. If, after a set period, the Lone Worker had not logged back to the control centre, then an emergency procedure would be initiated. To test the procedure we logged out and did not log back in again after the prescribed hour. We returned to base and enquired about our invocation of the emergency procedure. Nothing had been done and there was no formal record of the call: *We thought someone was mucking about.*

No procedure is worth anything unless it is agreed and adhered to.

The Lone Worker may well consider that his or her own 'issues' are in a way static and manageable, for example the insurance woman may accept that the area is unsuitable for her work. But there is still the final variable – the public itself. With every precaution and care, the Lone Worker will still have to deal with the public and some people are aggressive and seem to be looking for trouble. We are advocating a very simple basic strategy for Lone Workers.

- We need to act prudently all the time. Sensible behaviour should be automatic. Think of working to safe procedures as putting on a safety belt in a car – it should be a matter of fact and not a matter of being brave, foolhardy or cowardly.
- We need to think beforehand about any novel situation and be prepared to act accordingly.
- We need to be fully aware of any situation WE think is high risk and err on the side of caution, not bravery. We are not in the business of getting medals – remember that medals are inclined to be awarded posthumously and usually record success rather than bravery anyway.
- We need to monitor every situation and recognise when what is normally safe has the signs of getting out of hand.

The principle of the 'traffic lights'

We would like to introduce the analogy of a traffic light in classifying situations – an analogy we first met when training hotel staff in customer care. The waiters were asked to grade customers as they came into the dining area:

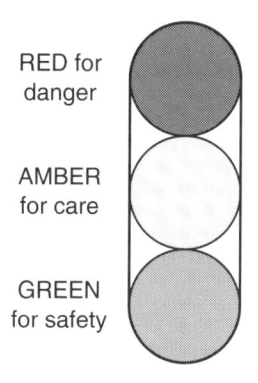

Figure 5.2

GREEN customers were people who, at a particular moment in time, would not give any trouble and were unlikely to complain except in the grossest of situations. Green customers would be expected to enjoy sharing a joke and if necessary could be asked to wait and be given less than the best tables.

RED customers were predictably 'trouble' and the Head Waiter would always need to be informed when they entered the restaurant. Predictable Red customers included food inspectors and, in the case of the hotel staff we were training, showbusiness people with their managers and agents. All drunks were classified a Red automatically.

AMBER customers presented the problems. Sometimes Amber customers were simply new people to the restaurant but other times they were well-known and usually Green customers in different situations.

A Mr Green and his partner were regular diners and enjoyed sharing the little politics of the hotel. On this occasion Mr Green turned up with a new partner and they were both shown to the usual table.

'*I do hope Mrs Green is not unwell?*', enquired the waiter. '*I am Mrs Green*', replied the new partner.

Amber customers and situations can change to red very quickly. The interaction between the Lone Worker, in our case, the situation and the individual can well produce some explosive chemistry. This will be the subject of Chapters 6 and 7.

Recognising Red situations is the first essential. A chemist working alone in a laboratory is a Red situation and it is recognised as such by the recommendations of the Health and Safety at Work Act. Dealing with a known dangerous patient is also always Red. These and many other situations, which the reader will be able to identify, are always clearly Red and will be special cases. The problem lies with the fringe areas – the Ambers.

However, situations can change. Nothing can be assumed to remain as it is. Whole districts can change from Green to Red and occasionally reverse the process.

Up to quite recently it was regarded that midwives were rarely the subject of violent attacks. This apparently green situation changed suddenly. A section of the public had come to realise that midwives carried drugs with a high street value.

A large multi-storey urban wasteland was reallocated from what were predominantly single parent families to pensioners' flats. Previously the Royal Mail had been very concerned over the delivery of Giros. Under the new allocation to the pensioners the flats became a much sought-after walk.

Situations are not general. The insurance collector in the Lamplugh movie estimated the collection of monies in the urban wasteland as being Red for her.

Amber means handle with care, and understand what is likely to make Green turn to Amber. The Ambers present the major challenges to management in that they demand continuous monitoring. In our view the fact that one worker – the Lamplugh insurance collector will do as an example – regards a situation as Red could well be valuable information of a trend. She *might* be a special case and no general action needs to be taken. She is much more likely to be signalling that the lights are changing for everyone in the area.

Exercise 5.1

Think of your own job and consider Green, Amber and Red situations.

Think of Green parts of your work – the people and situations where you are secure. List six criteria that you have used to categorise things as Green. Do these criteria apply to other people who might be qualified to do your work should you not be available?

Think of Red parts of your work – the people and situations where you are very much on your guard. List six criteria that you have used to categorise things as Red. What precautions do you take and are these adequate? Do others know of the situations? If the answer to the last two questions is not a definitive YES, who do you need to inform and what needs to be done?

Think of a Green situation turning to Amber. What factors made the Green situation turn to Amber and potentially Red? List these factors in a grid such as the one below, dividing them into the following categories; material factors; factors concerned with the other person or persons; and factors concerned with me.

Material factors	Factors concerned with the other person or persons	Factors concerned with ME

Looking at other lists from other jobs we can see a pattern. George is a mental care assistant and his list of factors that moved a Green situation to Amber and even Red looked like this for him:

Material factors	Factors concerned with the other person or persons	Factors concerned with ME
Dress – somehow white smocks give confidence	Jealousy	Looking rushed
Noise	Frustration	Talking down
Loss of possessions	Illness – discomfort generally	Not listening – not giving attention
Change of position, room, seat . . .		Showing anger or dislike
Disruption of TV		Clumsiness
Breaks in routine		
Medication		

The material factors carry a great deal of weight but the factors that concern George and his attitudes may surprise the reader. George is recognising that he has a major input into making Green situations turn to Amber or Red. It is not just OTHER people, we can BEHAVE OURSELVES INTO DANGER.

In the next chapter we will look at these factors and discuss their importance.

6

Behaving yourself into trouble

Messages, messengers and shadows – Elements others see of the messenger: preconceptions, physical characteristics, dress, words and the language we use, non-verbal behaviour – The total communication package – Showing empathy – Planning for effective communication.

In the last chapter we explained that the situations within the working life of the experienced Lone Worker could be classified as Green (basically safe), Red (intrinsically dangerous) and Amber (problematical and where for various reasons things could get awkward or positively dangerous). In this chapter we will look at some of the ways in which Lone Workers may inadvertently provoke aggression, driving a Green situation to Amber or pushing an Amber situation into Red, with the threat of violence when communicating with a client or member of the public. We will also look how many of the potential movements towards aggression can be avoided by 'structuring' a meeting.

Messages, messengers and shadows

It is impossible in face-to-face communication to deliver a *message* without in some way delivering ourselves, the *messenger*. With the messenger comes what may be called a shadow containing his or her attitudes both to the message and, most importantly, to the person to whom the message is intended. Messages, messengers and their shadows are viewed simultaneously by colleagues, bosses, subordinates, clients, customers

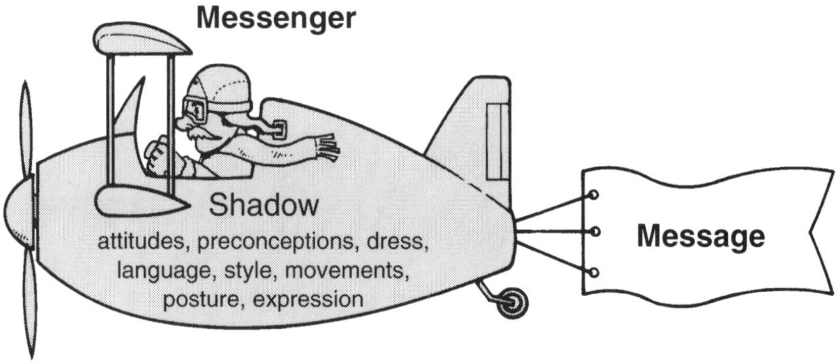

WORKING ALONE

Figure 6.1 We also deliver ourselves when we deliver a message

and contacts and the *total* package is judged as being either positive or negative. We will find that how we are perceived, how we present ourselves and how we behave are often more important in determining how our message is received than the substance of the message itself.

If the total communication – message and messenger together – is perceived as positive, then Green situations will remain safe and Amber will not be tipped to Red. If the total communication is perceived as being negative, then the Lone Worker may well be in danger.

Face-to-face communications contain two inseparable elements – the message and the messenger.

By watching the messenger and the shadow others deduce how the messenger feels about the message and more importantly *how the messenger feels about them.*

The perception others have of the messenger, virtually regardless of the message he or she carries, will determine the likelihood of a positive or a negative response

THE MESSAGE

The single point we are going to make here is that the substance of the message within our face-to-face communication needs to be clear and as simple as possible.

- Split down a complex message into simple steps.
- Give the steps priority.
- Take them one at a time.
- Make sure that each issue is settled and understood before proceeding.
- Leave when you are winning.

If you don't know where you are going you will finish up somewhere else.

MESSENGERS AND SHADOWS

The messenger has certain unavoidable characteristics that may determine his or her reception and acceptance.

- **Preconceptions.** All but the most open minded have some form of preconceptions of what people holding various offices *should* look like and talk like. If the Lone Worker does not meet these preconceptions then there is an immediate communications barrier that needs to be overcome. Sometimes the mis-match between the preconceptions and the reality are in the Lone Worker's favour, for example where a policeman is jovial and not stern, but it is always an issue.
- **Physical characteristics.** Colour, gender, height, etc. Remember that certain characteristics can at least be partially controlled.
- **Dress.** Although we cannot usually modify our physical appearance, we can modify the way we present ourselves.
- **Words and language.** Words are often far from neutral. The way we string words together – our language – often provides clues to our class and potential attitudes.
- **Non-verbal behaviour.** The portmanteau phrase for the minutiae of ways that we present ourselves, for example by our gestures, eye movement, pausing, stance, etc. People are able, with varying degrees of accuracy, to judge our attitudes towards them and our message by watching us.

Our shadow is composed of our physical presence, the language we use and the actual words we utter plus a myriad of non-verbal behaviours.

The shadow communicates, with some accuracy, our attitudes and feelings towards what we are saying and to whom we are speaking.

If people accept our shadow as being positive, then they are likely to have a positive approach to what we are saying. If they are suspicious or openly hostile to our shadow, then they are likely to be hostile to us and our message, regardless of our intentions.

Let's take a more detailed look at the elements of our shadow.

Preconceptions

A number of school children were asked to describe a senior manager, and their answers showed a surprising consensus:

The senior manager described by the school children was above average height (about 6ft 1ins tall) and was in his early to mid-40s. He was of average build, clean shaven with greying hair. He wore glasses and a dark three-piece suit with black shiny shoes. Somehow he looked like Bill Clinton.

The description is bad luck for both your authors, one of whom has a beard, is of average height and does not even own a three-piece suit. It is worse news for our other author who is female and well below average height. Both of us have been managers in large organisations.

If you have the physical characteristics expected of a figure in authority it is easier to be in control. If you look acceptable, then being accepted is easier. If, however, your physical presence stirs some prejudice or misconception in the mind of those with whom you have to communicate, then communication is going to be that much more difficult and perhaps hazardous. Your physical and unavoidable features are a significant part of your shadow. Many people have views on what the bearers of messages should look like and this can give rise to some very difficult and potentially hazardous situations.

We have one example of a Lone Worker who nearly assaulted a client in his own factory. Mary was an senior auditor of Afro-Caribbean origin. She was visiting a large factory with her male white subordinate and they were welcomed by the Managing Director to meet the Board.

'*Oh*', he said to her assistant, '*I was expecting two of you*'.

Physical characteristics

Perhaps related to preconceptions, physical characteristics do affect how we are received by others. Colour, age and gender are the most obvious but by no means the only characteristics outside our personal control that seem to prejudice our reception. Any form of physical disability seems to prejudice many people for or against us and can transform situations from safe to hostile.

Dress

It could be difficult to change your height, colour, age or gender according to the message you wish to put over. However, it is possible to dress appropriately.

The 'lucky' Lone Worker is provided with a suitable uniform, for example firemen, ambulance and postal delivery staff, police, etc., are people identifiable in their roles because of their uniforms. Alan, our insurance agent, has a form of uniform in that he is expected to wear a dark suit, but many Lone Workers need to choose versions of 'uniform' for themselves.

We met a man we had vaguely met before in an outdoor clothing store and he asked our advice. What did we think of a particular anorak he was trying on? Our answer was suitable vague, not the least because we had no idea what he did or indeed how he expected us to respond. We said it was 'quite nice' and got him to explain the problem.

Our acquaintance was a senior inspector for a national children's charity and he wanted the coat for everyday winter wear. His problem was that he wanted functional weather-proof clothing that would not intimidate the people of very limited means that were often his clients *and* not bring the charity into disrepute with the councillors and occasional 'media people' that he inevitably met in his job. It had at worst *not* to give any of the wrong messages to either groups.

The first anorak was in our opinion functional but a little flashy. It was also a 'little young' for him. Another coat came over as *looking* expensive and yet another gave the right messages but was hardly durable enough for the all-weather conditions he described to us. The anorak he finally chose was by far the most expensive in the shop and had what we can only describe as 'style'. It did not shout for attention but had a quiet quality. The ideal anorak would not give messages of superiority or trendiness downward or 'left-wing intellectual' to the people who, although not his 'clients', did in practice control his budget.

The words and the language we use

Logical people can be forgiven for assuming that the words, carefully chosen, will convey their intended message. Carefully chosen words are indeed more likely to convey their intended meaning than those chosen in the heat of emotion, but even the most carefully chosen words often carry their own shadow.

Many words have the nuances of class, background and age built into them. The 1982 edition of *Roget's Thesaurus*, for example, lists 33 words for a toilet, ranging from the common 'bog' to the genteel 'loo', the gross 'thunder-box' to the embarrassed 'rest-room'. The simple act of asking directions to the nearest convenience or comfort station, says many things about you, and certainly are seen by many as an indicator of social standing.

Apart from 'saying things about you', individual words themselves can actually raise the temperature of a communication. The obvious examples are the words that are the front line of racial, religious or sexual issues. Less obvious are the words that seem to go in and out of fashion, the use of 'black' and 'coloured' are examples. Such politically loaded words simply need care. Other words seem to have different standing in different communities – it is evidently seen to be a compliment to describe a child as a 'little bugger' in some areas, but not so in many other places.

The simple rules are:

- use simple words and do not try and show off by jokes of any kind until you are very sure of the situation.
- People are people and once you begin to classify them in clusters – blacks, whites or purples – you have a chance of offending.

We have discussed individual words, but innocent words constructed into apparently innocent structures in language are also part of our shadow. Reading and comparing the vocabulary of *The Times*, the *Daily Mirror* and the *Guardian* in covering the same story can provide an insight into appropriate language. The danger for the Lone Worker is that by 'editing' his or her language for a particular audience he or she may fall into the trap of talking down to an audience and appearing as patronising. The perception that you are talking down invites aggressive response. Lone Workers should be very aware of the language they use, especially the language that makes assumptions. Compare the messages and the shadows in Table 6.1.

Be aware of the language we use and as we will say again and again – *keep it simple and check for understanding.*

Beyond structure, the language we use may reveal our attitudes as surely as if we wrote them on a hoarding.

Table 6.1

Message – what is said	Shadow – what may be heard
Would you like me to explain slowly.	I am better than you – I understand these things because I have a degree.
We don't deal with that here.	You are too old, too young, etc., for my concern.
Shall I come back when your husband is in?	Because you are a woman, you do not have the right to make household decisions.
That's not the way we do it.	You are not one of *us*.

In this section we need to say something about diction. If people cannot hear or understand you, it may well lead to hostility. Again, keep it simple and never be ashamed to ask for clarification.

Exercise 6.1

Think of the words and phrases that annoy you when you are on the 'other end' of an encounter. How many of these words do you find yourself slipping into using?

The lists we have collected in the past can be classified into the following categories: élitist, ageist, racist, sexist and miscellaneous. We hesitate to include too many in the text for fear of enraging the reader.

Non-verbal behaviour

Up until now we have seen the shadow as coming from the physical presentation of messengers and the words they use, but probably the most trusted part of our shadow is what jargon calls 'non-verbal behaviour'. In the real world of face-to-face communication words are presented by people who smile, grimace, look away, blush, fold their arms, fuss with their watch straps, and all the myriad of other non-verbal signals.

Exercise 6.2

Listen to a politician who does not usually represent your views explaining how there is nothing to fear from a particular threat to our world. Assuming that you do not have a direct reason for disbelief, what would you take as indicators – the shadow – that he or she was sincere or insincere?

If you look at the words you have listed in Exercise 6.2, you will probably find it contains words like 'shifty'. Ask yourself what behaviour led you to use the word 'shifty'? You will probably be able to break down 'shifty' to include particular eye movements – too short or too prolonged stares – tightening of the facial muscles, the 'wrong' way of clasping the hands together, etc. We are constantly making decisions about people and what they say using such indicators. These indicators are the shadows that the politician and indeed every one of us carries with us *all* the time.

A final but very important part of our non-verbal behaviour is our use of *distance*. All of us have a area of personal space that we resent being invaded.

Exercise 6.3

When you are having a meal with a friend facing him or her across a table, invade their space. Push your glass across the invisible line dividing the table or, if you are being very cheeky, lay a paper or book 'on their side'. Watch the response.

We suspect that the glass will be delicately returned and the book or paper may even excite negative comment. We all like our space.

Space is also important on a micro level. Touching other people, for whatever reason must always be treated with care and it is always important to keep a social distance. The social distance varies with ethnic origin and what is acceptable for, say, a Northern European culture may be seen as much too close or threatening for someone whose roots were in the Indian sub-continent.

- *Never, as a Lone Worker, invade other people's territory:*
  - Is it all right for me to come in?
  - May I put my things on your table?
  - I got a little wet, is it OK for me to take off my coat?
- *Presume nothing – in anyone else's territory you are, at best, a guest.*
- *Err on the side of distance – until you know better.*

Giving bad news is never going to be easy. Giving bad news while you are presenting what is perceived by your audiences as being a negative shadow is downright dangerous.

The total communication package

The total communication package is the combination of the message, the messenger and the shadow. The important issue is that the message *and* the messenger's personal shadow are inseparable and are perceived by our audience together, but somehow the shadow usually gets the highest weighting in determining how our communications are received.

An out-patient hospital receptionist who had been verbally abused by a patient was observed over a day's work. An example of her work included the following dialogue.

Could I see the Doctor please?
   (The registration form is completed efficiently but without humour. The receptionist does not look up.)
We have a 'time of arrival priority system' – TAPS for short – here. This is your number and the time you registered.
   (The paper is handed over with the right hand and a cursory glance. The left hand continues with some work it is doing.)
When you are seen the time is checked and entered into a computer for our records. The seats are over there.
   (The receptionist waves briefly in the direction of the seated queue but does not really look up.)
How long will it be?
I'm not allowed to say.
   (Said in a firm way and catching the eyes of the patient firmly but looking away before the second part of the speech is delivered.)

If you sit over there the Doctor will see you as soon as she is available.
(Turns away to speak to someone else in the office.)

Delay of about 20 minutes.

Look, I have to get back to work. How long will it be?
The Doctor will see you when she is available. You will have to wait your turn.
(A strong and prolonged look at the patient with the hands grasped together on the desk.)
Wouldn't it be possible to see a nurse – it's not very serious.
You will have to wait your turn. Everyone does. Now if you will get back to your seat I will be able to get on with my work.
(She huffs loudly and gets on with her work.)

Listening and watching several such encounters the surprise was that she was not verbally or even physically assaulted by every patient. Everything she said and did seemed to encourage anger, it was a very hostile shadow which somehow completely outweighed the message she was attempting to get over. One felt that if she was giving away gold bricks, you would still have been resentful and angry.

We could probably all relive the conversation between the receptionist and the patient to be less provoking but still realistic – the message has to contain the reality of the queue, that the hospital is busy and that the Doctor needs to see patients before they receive any treatment. Lets re-mix the cocktail of the shadow without changing the message:

Could I see the Doctor please?
(Filling in of registration form, pausing to the patient's uncertainty over his Doctor and smiling about an old joke as he fills in the details of his age.)
Is this your first time in this hospital?
(Closing the form, filing it and giving the patient her full attention.)
Yes, well anyway since it got modernised.
Quite an improvement isn't it.
(Smile)
We now have a numbered waiting system. This card has a number and the time you came in. It helps us see that everyone is seen in order and checks on whether we are doing our job properly.
(She gives the form to the patient still holding a corner while he accepts it and points to the number and the time of arrival with her pencil. She waits until the patient has pocketed the form before continuing.)

The nurse will call out your number as soon as the Doctor is free.
How long will it be?
Its difficult for me to say, but you can see we are pretty busy. The Doctor will see you as soon as possible. There is a tea machine in the corner – it takes the new 10ps.
(She gives the patient full attention and smiles. As she mentions the vending machine she gestures to a small pile of change she has at the side of the desk.)

Delay of about 20 minutes.

Look, I have to get back to work. How long will it be?
(She keeps the patient's eye while she sorts her forms and then turns her back on him with one hand still on the desk.)
If you would like to go back to your seat I will try to find out.

Short delay.

(Eye clasping the patient firmly and matching his own concerned mood with the reply.)
Look, I am sorry, there has been an emergency case and it will be at least an hour before anyone can see you.
Wouldn't it be possible to see a nurse – it's not very serious.
(Measured firm tone looking at the patient all the time.)
That's not possible I am afraid, the Doctor needs to see everyone first.
(Softening tone.)
Would it help for you to phone? There is a coin box in the entrance.
I had better get back to work.
Sorry, I think you picked a bad day.
(Slight smile.)
It looks as if it's always a bad day here.
(The patient is smiling and the receptionist catches the smile and laughs.)
I think you are probably right.

The new conversation is not subversive. The substance is the same. The receptionist does not break any hospital procedures and the patient still does not get the treatment in the time he required. This was not within the constraints of the receptionist's world. However, we would suggest that both the receptionist and the patient left the encounter feeling quite good. In both cases the receptionist had completed the right hospital forms, directed the patient correctly and followed procedures. In both cases the patient left without treatment but we are certain that he would have interpreted what had been said to him in a different way.

In both cases the *shadow* of non-verbal behaviour was coherent but, in the first case, dismissive. The receptionist spoke and behaved as if the patient was a cypher – the unpleasant reality of what was otherwise a well-ordered job. This was the shadow that the patient would react against and hence be hostile to the message – that he could not be seen more quickly. In the second case the patient *was the job* and this involved treating him as a human being and empathising with his concerns but retaining a professional reality. Think also of the two alternative ways they explained that the patient would be seen in turn:

What is said	What is heard
The Doctor will see you as she is available.	The Doctor is important and you are not. She will try and fit you in.
The Doctor will see you as soon possible.	The Doctor is busy right now but wants to see you. You are important.

The slight change of phrasing moves the patient from being inferior to the doctor – a case of fitting in the patient when she is not actually busy with something more important – to a position where the patient is important and the very busy doctor wants to see him. The new shadow allowed a positive attitude to what was still a negative message. When she had got her point across she was able to smile sympathetically and leave what was, in fact, a dissatisfied customer with a good feeling. He did not like the message but went away with a positive attitude.

Showing empathy

At the end of the first meeting with the receptionist, the patient is likely either to accept a position of inferiority or to 'fight back' into self-respect. In the second case the patient is respected and can accept what is being said to him without feeling either inferior or rebellious. The patient has been understood and is able to leave understanding something of the receptionist's problems. It is the feeling of mutual empathy that allows the patient to accept the message in a positive way and hence he is much less likely to become angry, whatever the message he is being given.

By showing empathy the receptionist had allowed the patient to be empathetic back and reduced a potentially hostile situation. Genuine empathy is necessary since if we feign, the shadow will somehow come over as non-coherent and we will be seen as untrustworthy.

It is our belief that by showing empathy to others we become more 'human' to them and are thus less likely to be an object of their aggression.

If we do not empathise genuinely then the words we use and our non-verbal behaviour will not match and we will leave those we work with confused and distrustful.

HOW DO WE LEARN TO SHOW GENUINE EMPATHY?

The reader may remember Eileen, the pollution control officer in Chapter 4 who was shot at by a farmer while taking water samples on his land. Eileen was able to see the situation from the farmer's point of view. From that stand-point he took her to be a trespasser and acted accordingly. Seeing things from the other's point of view is a valuable technique for the Lone Worker who wishes to perform his or her job most efficiently and safely.

The technique is one of the tools we have borrowed from the work of Bandler and Grinder. These writers would see Eileen originally thinking in what they call the 'First Position'. We then asked Eileen to think of herself as the farmer. They would call this the 'Second Position'. However, Bandler and Grinder would argue that in both the First and Second Positions, Eileen was *involved* in the situation and a dispassionate overview was impossible. To obtain a dispassionate situation they advocate the use of a 'Third Position', almost like a fly on the wall watching the antics of the people below (*see* Fig 6.2).

BEHAVING YOURSELF INTO TROUBLE

How do I feel about them?

How do they feel about me?

How do they look? How do they sound?

First Position   **Second Position**

Third Position

Figure 6.2 Establishing empathy – the three positions

By using the technique of seeing things from this Third Position the Lone Worker can view a situation from a dispassionate viewpoint. From this position Eileen could see that she was being emotional about her job and the farmer about his land. In the Third Position, acting almost in the role of a film director trying to make a film where everyone wins, she can make major adjustments to her approach or, in our jargon, her shadow.

Using the 'Third Postion' technique, emotion can also be seen for what it may well be – a dangerous way of turning the lights from Green to Red. The application of the technique may seem laborious or indeed 'odd'. We can only say that it works and has worked with people who have been very sceptical initially. Let us suppose we are working with our receptionist.

First, we would get her to role play her contacts with what she saw as an awkward patient by being herself in what we call the First Position. We would ask her go through the conversation in her head and then we would ask her to take the part of the patient, in the Second Position. In this position she would attempt to say what she had heard, seen and felt about the way the receptionist had 'behaved'. Hopefully she would take in the patient's perception of the message and the shadow. Returning to her role as the receptionist in the First Position, and moving physically in the room, she would be asked to

95

modify her approach to avoid some of the negatives that had been identified.

It is unusual to find that behaviour will change so simply. Usually it is necessary to attempt to call in an outsider's view, that is someone who has none of the prejudices and apprehensions of seeing it from his or her own perspective. The outsider's viewpoint we call the Third Position and we achieve it by moving the 'client' (in this case the receptionist) some distance – about three metres – from where she has been practising the First and Second Positions. The Third Position is designed to be free of emotion.

We would tell her, that from the vantage point of the Third Position, she is the director of a film about effective behaviour and that she is empowered to make any changes to the way the scene is being played.

In the First Position she will probably see things very much as they were – an arrogant patient who does not understand the problems of the NHS. Hopefully, in the Second Position, she may recognise that the patient is uneasy and finds the whole aura of the hospital unsettling. The receptionist might, from the Third Position for example, realise that minor changes of the 'set' would help her in her work and reduce the potential hostility of the situation. Thus she might see that an 'in-tray' for the registration documents would assist her in moving from the formal role of bureaucrat to the more open role of getting the patient to wait. In the Third Position she might also realise that although she can see the vending machine from her desk, it is masked from the patient's view and that he perceives her directions as dismissive.

There are times when even getting 'clients' to establish themselves in the Third Position does not provide enough clues for effective working. In this case a Fourth Position, which we call the 'Producer', may work. The Producer is able to look upon the work of the First, Second and Third Positions and decide that they have all got it wrong. In our case of the receptionist, the Producer may decide that the whole siting of the desk in relation to the door is wrong or that the notices that direct patients to the reception are unclear. As one can see, such exercises can prove to be valuable learning experiences.

The next exercise provides the detailed instructions for taking someone through the procedures that we are recommending for establishing empathy using the three positions.

Exercise 6.4

Think of a difficult situation you are currently facing, for example an interview you are dreading with a difficult individual. Find yourself some space and lay out a scene as it will be when you meet the person. Think about whether you will be standing up, facing him or her across a desk, walking together, etc.

Get the whole scene of your encounter as you plan it now. Hear the person's voice and your own, see the person and feel how you think you will feel. Not necessarily out loud, 'say' what you plan to say to the other person. Now, move over to where the other person is and listen to what you have just heard. How do you respond? How do you feel about what you have just heard and seen? Still in the 'skin' of the second party, tell 'the first party' about your response and what you would have preferred to see and hear.

Move back to your own first position and hear what has just been said. Modify what you are going to say to meet the comments without losing the 'meat' of the message. As the second party, and moving accordingly, hear and respond again.

Now think of the scene between the two people as being a film you are making about the Lone Worker – the person facing the difficult meeting. The film has to show the Worker in a favourable light. Move about three metres from where the two 'players' have just been and play back the scene in your head. What could you do to improve matters and make sure that the message was conveyed effectively and efficiently?

Planning for an effective communication

Most of the time the communications we make are natural and in our jargon, that is they are Green situations. However, Amber and Red situations need more care. We are suggesting that for such situations we take a step back and plan carefully.

Let us imagine we are preparing for a difficult meeting.

THE MESSAGE

The message often has two elements: the professional message, the essential information that you need to convey, and the secondary message. The secondary message often contains what you would like to get over. Taking our receptionist as a model, for example, she has to get over the information that the patient cannot be seen immediately but she would also like to get over the secondary point that it would be a good idea to wait.

The receptionist needs to consider what is the essential core of the message, and if she fails to get this over, to abandon the secondary message.

It is also important to accept the concept that we, as messengers, have an inevitable shadow that may determine the reception of our message and that by consciously attempting to empathise with the 'client' we may increase the chances of being seen in a positive light. Looking at the issue dispassionately it may be possible to see how aspects of the 'messenger's shadow' may be modified. It may even be possible to use what we termed the 'Fourth Position' to see that, however well we try, we are not the right messenger.

Rule 1: Be clear of your message and its purpose. Consider the likely reception.of your message.

PLAN TACTICS

Everyone, to a greater or lesser extent, needs to know the boundaries of the communication and the roles of the people present. In Chapter 4 we discussed the problems and risks that role ambiguity brought to the Lone Worker. Here we are suggesting that any communication/meeting should involve, as a second step, a clear and honest statement to remedy any possible misconceptions.

'My name is PC West, this is my warrant card. I am here to investigate reports of an incident outside the Bay Horse on Tuesday last.'

'My name is John East and I am a representative of Bloggo Software. I would like to show you the latest version of the computer program you are already using.'

'I am a representative of National Rivers Authority and I am investigating a reported pollution incident.'

'Hello, I have a recorded delivery for you. Would you mind signing here.'

All cases would be improved by the formal showing of identification and some form of publicly recognised uniform.

Decide on your role. Looking back on the incident of Eileen, the pollution control officer, we may remember that she could adopt any one of the roles, detective, adviser or enforcer, and that each role demanded different behaviour. In looking at our message, we may see that the essential message requires a different role from the optional or secondary message. We need to be very clear on how we indicate our change of role or the client may become confused.

Along with our planning of the tactics we need to think about how we are able to tell whether we are moving from the Green situation to an Amber one or from the Amber situation to a Red one. We have to be aware that we may not be getting across.

Rule 2: Agree roles and agenda.

PREPARE FOR CONTINGENCIES

In a potentially dangerous or difficult situation we need to stick by the letter of the law in our safety procedures.

Rule 3: For potentially difficult meetings, plan ahead. Select your role and attempt to empathise with the recipient of the message. Work on the positive factors that you, the messenger, can bring to the situation and reduce the negative factors.

MAINTAIN EMPATHY

For communication to be truly effective you will need to maintain empathy with your client. The best way to achieve this is to match the mood of the other person.

I was managing a small group of salespeople who had to sell ideas and concepts to senior managers of companies associated with my own. I received a telephone call from a very irate manager, whom, in the terminology of the last chapter, I had always regarded as 'green'. He was normally easy going and very helpful to my side of the business.

'If you send that young pup round again you can forget business with me.'
'John? I'm sorry about that. Can you give me any idea . . . ?'
'Just about everything – attitude, attitude will do.'

The 'young pup', John, was a new graduate who was very enthusiastic about his job. His reading of the meeting was that he had presented his portfolio and had simply been thrown out.

We made him role play exactly what happened and I understood. The manager was sitting back in his chair in a very relaxed way and John had *bounced* him. There was no ice-breaking conversation about hold-ups on the motorway. He had refused the offer of a coffee on the grounds that he was in a hurry and he had put his briefcase on the manager's desk and started to sell to him without bothering about any of the social niceties. John was faced with a relaxed manager who had probably had a hard day.

John could well have been faced with an exactly opposite situation. The manager could have been between meetings and just able to fit John in. In such a situation John's bouncing style might have been exactly right and an insistence to go through the niceties of coffee and hold-ups on motorways would have aroused just as much anger. The professional communicator has to match the mood of the time or expect aggression.

On a very physical level impatience is easy to spot as well as sense. Somebody who is in a hurry is inclined to work in short gestures – they are likely be standing or perhaps sitting on the edge of the chair. It will be impossible to obtain the person's complete concentration for any extended period of time and there are likely to be interruptions. You can sense whether people are relaxed or tense very easily. The gestures will be sweeping but sedate, John would have been brought into the room and not, as would have been the case of the 'hurry' situation, indicated where to sit by someone who was not really looking at him. The voice patterns are also a clear guide and the key to handling the situation most effectively. If the delivery is slow, match that delivery. If the delivery is staccato, match that as well. With training it is possible to learn how to pace your delivery with the others and very gently move the pace so that you meet your own needs.

Never make any sudden change of pace until you feel that the situation is firmly 'Green'.

Every new meeting must be treated as Amber at best.

The very simple thing that John could have done to check the pace the manager wished to maintain was to ask: 'How long have we got?'

It is very important to recognise the *pace* of the other person's world. If you miss the pace of the person you are speaking to, you will annoy them.

Judging mood, pacing as we shall call it, is the first skill that the Lone Worker needs to acquire to complete any successful communication.

Rule 4: Judge the mood of people you have to communicate with and attempt to match it. Watch out for the clues that what you are doing is not working and be prepared to be flexible.

Having established a formal agenda and the roles of the parties in it, and having recognised the importance of maintaining empathy, the communication can continue.

Professional message *(what* must *be conveyed or the meeting fails)*	***Secondary message*** *(what we or the organisation would* like *to convey in addition, provided the primary message is accepted*
My name is PC West, this is my warrant card. I am here to investigate an incident outside the Bay Horse on Tuesday last.	Look Mrs Hickson, I know that it has been a shock to you. If you like I could arrange for a WPC to visit you later.

My name is John East and I am a representative of Bloggo Software. I would like to show you the latest version of a computer program we have developed.	I realise that we did not sell you the other software you are using but I could look and see if I could . . .
I am a representative of the National Rivers Authority and I am investigating a reported pollution incident.	I accept that you have a problem but we are not responsible for storm drains. However, if you like I can give you a contact in the local council who will be able to offer advice.
Hello, I have a recorded delivery for you.	Yes, I am wet and would love a cup of tea.

As the reader may guess, the increased risk in meeting comes through the secondary message. However, it may also be the case that the secondary message is personally important to the Lone Worker. Again there is a question of balancing risk.

The basic rules of safe and effective communication

- Always remember that the signals you convey by the simple act of being there – your shadow – are often more significant in determining the way your message is received than the message itself. *Get it wrong and you will have 'behaved' yourself into trouble.*
- Treat people as human beings; what do they want to know?; what is unclear and what do they need?
- Always be polite.
- Use simple and concise language.
- Put yourself in the others position: how do they see me?; is this how they should see me?
- Question whether your non-verbal signals match the message your words intend to give out.
- Pace your communication to match that of the 'client'.
- Deal with your professional objectives before you even consider moving onto other issues, however important they are to you personally.

In this chapter we have touched briefly on the issues of the '-isms' – sexism, racism, ageism, éliteism. For unwary Lone Workers the '-isms' can provide traps which may trigger unfortunate responses from clients, even when the Lone Workers feel they are acting professionally. In the next chapter we will develop this point and look at how we can review our prejudices when they are likely to impede our effective and safe working.

7

I can hear what you say but I can see what you mean

Attitude problems – The Attitude Loop: using the STOP sign – Reviewing faulty internal dialogue – Classifying faulty internal dialogue: the Ellis Belief Systems – 6 types of 'bad' attitudes – Resisting pressure: playing the ball and not the person, Broken Record, Fielding, Workable Compromise – Dealing with criticism: Appropriate Assertion and Constructive Enquiry – Giving criticism – Guidelines to constructive feedback – Professional distancing.

In the previous chapter we discussed the complexity of human face-to-face communication. We saw that no messenger can deliver a message without delivering something of him or herself as well. We saw that others observe the messenger and judge from the cocktail of signals that he or she gives out, how they will react. People to whom we communicate judge the total process of communication, often giving much more weight to the messenger than the message. If the total process is perceived as:

- positive, then they are likely to be more positive to the message and its messenger.
- negative, then they are more likely to be negative to the message and its messenger.
- mis-matched – for instance if the bringer of bad news smiles too much – then the recipients are inclined at least to be confused and untrusting.

I CAN HEAR WHAT YOU SAY BUT I CAN SEE WHAT YOU MEAN

We then discussed ways in which the process of delivering the message can be improved and how the messenger can increase the likelihood of being seen positively by empathising with the client, planning difficult situations and by such mechanical things as dressing suitably. Overall we were talking about other people's attitudes towards us. In this chapter we will take one step back and discuss how our attitudes to other people can catalyse their attitudes towards us. People recognise the pattern of behaviours that we have termed 'mis-matched' as showing attitudes towards them. They sense us as not being genuine and resent it. We will begin by demonstrating that people are very good at picking up and analysing our attitudes, however much we may attempt to hide them. We will then look at ways of stopping to review our attitudes and hopefully coming out with more acceptable ones.

Attitude problems

Kevin was a lecturer in English at a small town technical college. His background was of a minor public school and his father-in-law was a judge. As far as anyone could tell he was a good teacher, diligent and careful. He hated the job and he despised the students but as he often said:

'Look, I do the job well and I never give out any signals that they are rubbish. If I taught a mainline subject, something they could use, it would be fine, but they all regard English as a waste of time. They are on day release and they have to take it and I have to teach it.'

The local press made quite a thing of it when he was attacked by a group of his students in the town main street and put into hospital. And he thought he never gave out any signals that he thought *they* were rubbish.

If we consider the lecturer from the local technical college who was assaulted by several of his pupils in the High Street of his home town, the message – his classwork and much of the detail of his presentations – were probably similar to those used by thousands of teachers who do not get assaulted by their pupils. The messenger caused the pupils to understand and resent his attitudes towards them. Can we avoid others understanding our *attitudes*?

Exercise 7.1

In the company of a few colleagues, ask one of them (preferably not someone you know intimately) to let you try an experiment. The experiment is to show that lying is impossible.

First ask the 'guinea pig' to think of someone they dislike, or do not get on with. Do not get them to identify the 'disliked' individual but get them to attempt to see the individual in their mind's eye and, if possible, hear them talk in their imagination.

Then ask them to think of someone whom they like and get on with well. Again get them to visualise the 'liked' person and hear them talk.

While they think of the two people, watch them very carefully – see the eye movement, look out for slight changes in tension round the mouth or stiffening of facial muscles generally. Get them to repeat the visualisation several times until you can recognise the pattern, but do not be thrown out by gross visual expressions – grins or grimaces. What you are looking for are very slight movements that happen every time.

Now, provided the 'guinea pig' has taken the exercise seriously and has actually thought of real people (check this out before you proceed) you can go on with the experiment. Ask them to think of the taller (the older, or better dressed, etc) person and watch the face.

Most of the time you will be able to identify whether they are thinking of the 'friend' or the 'foe'. The minute eye movements or muscle contractions are a complete giveaway.

Obviously the experiment is not 100 per cent successful, but it works sufficiently often for us to be able to deduce that we can determine a great deal about people's thinking without them saying a word.

If we have a negative attitude towards particular people, it shows in our face, whatever we say to the contrary.

This very simple concept has a considerable effect on our communications with others because it determines the relationship almost from the first instant of contact. What is happening in our heads is that we think about things and people and our thoughts are allowed to generate feelings which affect our behaviour in the subtle ways that we noticed in the

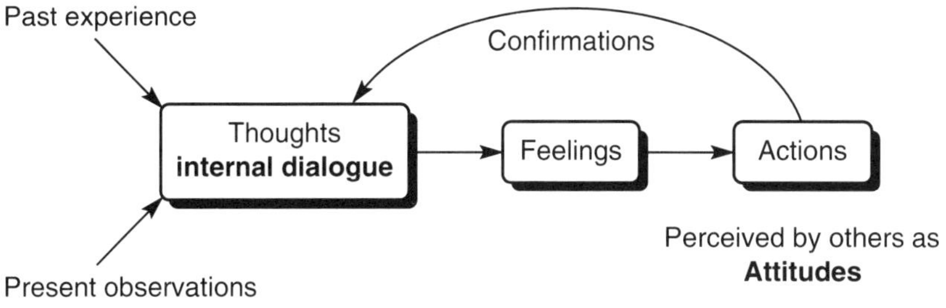

Figure 7.1 The Attitude Loop

experiment – the subtle changes in our posture, facial expression, movements, etc. Once we have the feelings, they are not under our control. Obviously some people do not demonstrate their feelings as strongly as others – the 'poker faces' exist, but none of us can completely hide our feelings. We are used to looking for clues of people's feelings in their faces and often in their eyes. This is why we may find that dark glasses seem hostile and why people with eye defects – squints or even glass eyes – are difficult to communicate with. The eyes are 'mirrors to the soul' – if we let them be.

The Attitude Loop

Take the case of the teacher, Kevin. When he approached his class he found it difficult not to think of himself as being superior to the students and this *internal dialogue* blocked his logical thinking. Without the internal dialogue blocking his sensible thought he would have been able to think of the class he saw before him at least as being 'his job' or at least human beings for whom he had responsibility. However, his thoughts were on 'yobbos' and he felt bad about having to work with 'yobbos'. His past experience – the way he was brought up to despise such people by his parents – originated his *negative* internal dialogue and the way the class behaved on a day-to-day basis reinforced his thinking. The class did all the things that he expected 'yobbos' to do and the fact that they knew he despised them encouraged them to act even more outrageously, culminating in the assault. This sequence of thoughts and associations is known as the Attitude Loop (*see* Fig 7.1).

If we make the assumption that if we allow our thoughts to lead to feelings, then our actions will betray us, we need to rethink our thoughts *before* they lead to the feelings. We need to stop and review many of our thoughts before they overtake us and encourage us to act inappropriately and dangerously. If we cannot undertake the review, then the internal dialogue may well become so deafening that any possibility of rational, appropriate behaviour is impossible. If we do not review the relevance of our approach we may well get into some excess of behaviour – a catastrophic spiral. In order to avoid getting into the spiral we need to block our thoughts and review them *before* they lead to feelings. Once feelings are involved the process is unstoppable: others detect our 'attitude' and very often resent it. Their process of resentment may well make our own feelings stronger and the spiral accelerates.

Employing assertive behaviour now is likely to provide the most effective way of lessening the effects of the catastrophe spiral. Acting assertively is acting appropriately from choice and may involve passive or aggressive behaviour – the most important issue is the element of choice. Passive attitudes may at best lose us our case and prevent us getting our message across or at worst invite bullying. Aggressive attitudes are likely to challenge aggressive responses. Our strategy to avoid passive or aggressive attitudes consists of:

- pausing to review our internal dialogue when we recognise it appearing;
- replacing, when appropriate, negative internal dialogue with sound dialogue; and
- being quite clear what is the purpose of our communication, i.e. understanding the substance of the message we wish to convey.

I CAN HEAR WHAT YOU SAY BUT I CAN SEE WHAT YOU MEAN

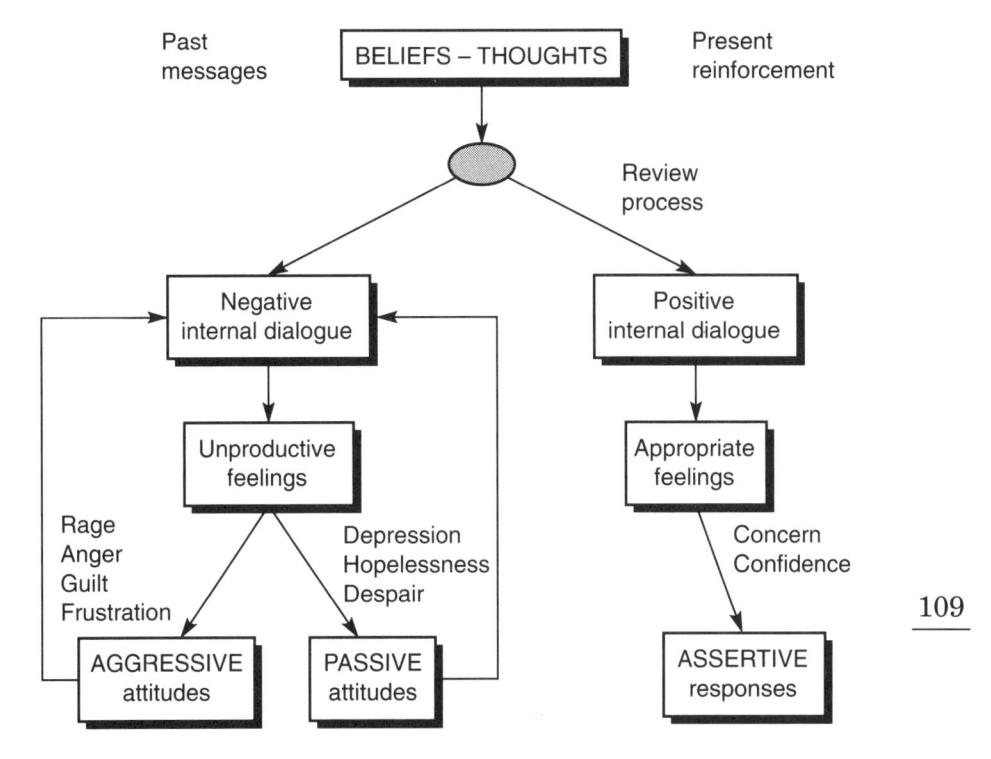

Figure 7.2 The thinking process

We will begin by a technique for stopping and reviewing our attitudes. We will then look at the process of replacing faulty with sound internal dialogue and then classify the dialogue itself. We will close by looking at a simple technique to avoid being 'wound up' and being pressured into faulty internal dialogue.

Stopping the Attitude Loop: use the STOP sign

Once we have begun to generate negative internal dialogue, the process of demonstrating our attitudes to others is under way. We have to say STOP to ourselves the instant non-productive thoughts come into our heads.

Patrick was brought up in a white suburb in South Africa and had never, until he moved to Europe, met any blacks on a peer basis. The problem became acute for him when he was on a training course run by a black PhD trainer. He found himself continuously uncomfortable and unable to concentrate on his work.

Patrick's problem was dealt with in three stages. The first stage was to get Patrick to verbalise his problem and then to recognise how his feelings were causing him real stress. The second stage was to get him to recognise when the prejudicial thoughts were beginning and to visualise a large STOP sign in front of him. Once he saw the STOP sign, the third stage was to make him review the dialogue in his head and replace it with more positive phrases.

Patrick was someone who perceived his world in visual terms and the STOP sign that caused him to review his prejudice was very clear to him – he saw it and was able to describe it in great detail. Not everyone perceives the world visually and variations of the STOP-sign technique have been developed. Some people prefer to imagine the *word* 'stop' being shouted at them from a distance while others like to feel themselves being trapped in some sort of quicksand when they have what they see as unproductive thoughts.

Reviewing negative internal dialogue

The negative internal dialogue that leads us to show what others see as a negative attitude towards them has roots in our past. For example, the thoughts we have are probably derived from attitudes we inherited from our childhood and have not brought up to date.

We remember a salesman who considerably annoyed a customer by rotating a horseshoe on his wall while they were waiting on the doorstep for payment. He explained that 'horseshoes the wrong way up drain out the luck'. Once he had said the phrase, and recognised that he was using his father's words, he felt very foolish.

Passivity. The response of someone acting on their negative internal dialogue. By passivity we mean the action of people who do not really feel that they have 'permission', from the 'important people' around them, to act for themselves. Such people accept the world as they perceive it, which is usually negatively. They constantly do what they think will gain them approval.

Having identified negative internal dialogue it is important to turn it around – to make it positive internal dialogue. Table 7.1 shows how some examples of negative internal dialogue have been reviewed into positive internal dialogue. Readers may like to complete the blank spaces

Table 7.1

Negative internal dialogue	Positive internal dialogue
I cannot change the way I behave – I am made this way.	Although it may well be difficult, I can change my behaviour.
I must be approved by everyone and I cannot risk disapproval by any action of mine. Thus, I cannot ask my neighbour to park more considerately, because I might offend them.	I would like to be respected by everyone, however I do not need such approval. If I am not respected by someone who is important to me, I can find out the reason and decide whether I can and wish to change my behaviour.
My emotional state is determined by external events – people, the weather – thus I have no real control over my feelings.	I accept that I am not perfect and that I can lose control at times. It is something that I am working on and I am improving.
I don't like the way things are developing but they are out of my control.	If I can't change what is happening, then it's frustrating I know. Basically, one has to make the best of things and move on from there.
I get fouled up by people who want things too quickly and it's their fault if I make mistakes.	I want to achieve what is realistic given what I understand is needed. If I am asked the impossible, it's up to me to negotiate.
I have a duty to stop other people doing things that I feel are wrong, whatever the situation.	I have the choice of intervening when others are doing something that has negative consequences, and in particular negative consequences for me directly.
Punish the guilty.	I have a choice of facilitating change but it may not work. You win some, you lose some.

Negative internal dialogue	Positive internal dialogue
This presentation will be a disaster. None of the equipment works.	
They have no right to catch me out like that. I should have been told.	
I must have all the correct answers. I have to look as if I know my stuff.	
I always hate going to this sort of party. Full of clever people who make me feel small.	
It's OK for them, they are white/male/older/more intelligent, etc.	
It's OK for them, they are prepared/better dressed/speak more fluently, etc.	
I will have to do it myself, as usual.	

Negative internal dialogue usually relates to the past. Messages in our heads tell us:

- that somehow we are wrong;
- that somehow we are inferior;
- how things and people should behave;
- how we ought to behave.

These messages have been classified by Albert Ellis, a respected psychologist.

Classifying negative internal dialogue

Albert Ellis, a respected psychologist, codified four belief systems that he considered caused 'nine-tenths of all human suffering'. It would be easy to imagine any of his belief systems in our faulty internal dialogue.

Belief System 1: an overall purpose for the Universe

The belief is that of an overall cosmic order of things extending to individual problems – *'God wouldn't let this happen'; 'It will be alright on the night'; 'It won't happen to me'*.

These three pieces of faulty dialogue from the first belief system are responsible for many Lone Worker incidents. They contribute to many worthy safety codes being ignored.

The following tables show examples of negative internal dialogue relating to Ellis' belief systems and some examples of how these thoughts can be turned into positive internal dialogue.

Negative internal dialogue	Positive internal dialogue
God wouldn't let this happen.	This is a real incident and it needs my immediate attention. The HOWs and WHYs can wait.
It will be alright on the night.	Let's do a full risk analysis and take appropriate action.
It won't happen to me.	!!!!!!!!!!!

Belief System 2: a fundamental belief in hierarchy

The belief is that the hierarchy of society will protect the individual – *'The company will protect me'; 'The boss knows best'*.

Negative internal dialogue	Positive internal dialogue
The company will protect me.	Under the Health and Safety at Work Act I, too, am responsible for my own safety.
The boss knows best.	Yes, if I tell him or her. I am on the ground and I, in this probably restricted area, know more about what is likely to be safe and what is likely to be dangerous than anyone alive.

Belief System 3: others should behave to our standards or beliefs

This set of beliefs encourage the manager of the Lone Worker to pass on assumptions about other people without checking and to draw unfavourable conclusions about them if they do not mind-read. They also lead to the recognisable attitudes that may lead directly to assaults. Examples are: *'These people seem to be incapable of filling in a form correctly or even spelling their names without prompting'; 'Others have my own high safety standards – the ladder will have been checked'; 'They ought to be able to stand on their own two feet – I can. Because I am strong and self-assured, other people should be'; 'Look, I'm in a hurry, why can't you get a move on . . .'; Why can't they be doing something useful'; 'They ought to be grateful that I'm out on a cold night protecting them.'*

The six statements above represent the six groupings of internal dialogue that seem to give rise to attitude problems. These are:

1. *Superiority* – the view that the individual or the group is somehow superior or inferior to others by right.

2. *Perfectionism* – any imperfections are fundamentally wrong and those making them are inferior in some way.

3. *Strength* – It is wrong to show any form of weakness and those showing weakness, or emotion, are inferior.

4. *Urgency* – somehow being in a rush and being dominated by the clock is the right state of affairs. Those who do not share our urgency are a nuisance.

5. *The work ethic* – somehow it is wrong not to be actively engaged in work whether it is useful or not. Those not busy are lazy and otherwise inferior.

6. *Helping* – We are in this world to help others whether they ask for or even need help. Those who are not grateful for our help or do not feel the same way about helping are not good people.

Unconsidered, all these attitudes can give rise to faulty internal dialogues that may well lead to violence.

Belief System 4: I must behave in a proscribed way to be a good person

Examples of Belief System 4 are: *'To be a good policeman I must never show any sign of weakness. Weakness means I am not up to the job'*; *'I know I am tired and am beginning to make mistakes, but the job must be completed today'*.

Belief System 4 is a curse we may well have inherited from well-meaning parents. The good life is somehow conditional on passing certain hurdles. If you do not conform to standards/ jump these hurdles, you have somehow failed, not just as standard/ hurdle jumper, but also as a human being. The failure is not simply in the performance but in your existence – to fail an exam is to deprive you of love in your parents' eyes.

The negative internal dialogues that the six clusters of Belief System 3 give rise to block our constructive thought and lead us to behaviours that others may recognise as hostile attitudes. It is important to identify and classify our internal dialogues and to replace them, as necessary, with more appropriate language and thus avoid potentially violent situations. Table 7.2 gives examples of more appropriate dialogue.

We will see later that the criticism of us by others can amplify our internal dialogue and increase the risks of being perceived as hostile.

Table 7.2

Attitude	Example of negative internal dialogue	Example of positive internal dialogue
Superiority is good. I am superior, you are not and are therefore inferior.	These people seem incapable of . . .	It is a bit of a nuisance to have to go over things, but I'll survive.

Attitude	*Example of negative internal dialogue*	*Example of positive internal dialogue*
Perfectionism is good. I strive for perfection, you do not and are therefore inferior.	Others will have the same high standards – the ladder will have been checked.	It's my life, I will make sure for myself. Ultimately it's my risk and my responsibility.
Strength is good. I am strong, you are not and therefore inferior.	Because I'm strong . . . They ought to be able to stand on their own two feet . . .	There is no connection between my skills and those of others. I'm lucky and hopefully can pass on my own experience. I still need to listen and understand.
Urgency is good, you do not accept that everything is urgent and therefore you are a nuisance	Look, I'm in a hurry, can't you see that. Get a move on.	I am in a hurry but in all honesty it has nothing to do with anyone else.
Work in itself is good. I work therefore I am superior.	Why can't they be doing something useful?	Obviously I can't see the point of what is going on but why should I be able to – it's none of my business.
Helping is good. You are not helping or grateful . . .	They ought to be grateful that I'm out on a cold night protecting them.	Some of them may well be, but they all have their own lives to live.

Exercise 7.2

Think of at least six situations where you found yourself not performing as you would have liked. (Examples from two situations we have met in the past are of a professional having difficulties explaining technicalities to his or her seniors in formal conditions, or perhaps attempting to explain to a colleague that they were taking undue risks.) Take a definite example, deciding what you were actually attempting to do.

Look back on your list and attempt to listen to the internal dialogues at the time. Did what you actually did come as a response to the internal dialogue or from your judgement of what was necessary?

To behave effectively we need to have time to review our internal dialogue and decide on relevant action. We must be able to give ourselves a pause.

Resisting pressure

'He kept on coming at me with excuses and finally I got angry – "Look, you know darned well that you can't park your car here, whatever make it is. Bloody move it!" That was when he started getting nasty'.

The Park Warden had allowed himself to get wound up by someone who came up with a range of excuses and finally lost his temper with unfortunate consequences. The technique he should have used – and we accept that it is easier to write about patience than practise it – is Broken Record.

'You are not permitted to park your car here sir. I have to ask you to move it.'
'Look, I will only be here for five minutes.'
'You are not permitted to park your car here sir. I have to ask you to move it.'
'Five minutes Warden!'
'You are not permitted to park your car here sir. I have to ask you to move it.'
'Is someone expected or something.'
'You are not permitted to park your car . . .
'I think you are being very unreasonable.'
'You are not permitted . . . '

The process of *not* having to think about the reply allows you the freedom of not beginning any internal dialogue on *having* to help, on *having* to get tough, on *having* to do anything.

Simply deciding on a position and redefining it *over* and *over* again does work. However, when deciding on what position you will take in a given situation you must remember to 'play the ball and not the person'; that is, your position should be determined by the *issue* at stake and not by the person or his attitudes. Avoid developing your own attitude problems. The Broken Record technique as it is known, is simple and does allow us time to review our position.

To resist pressure and buy time use the Broken Record technique. Decide on a position, use a level voice and do not be afraid to say the same thing over and over again. Do not be drawn and remember you do not need to answer questions.

However, the Broken Record technique alone is a trifle brisk and can be infuriating for the person on the receiving end. It can be softened by 'Fielding'.

'You are not permitted to park your car here sir. I have to ask you to move it.'
'Look, I will only be here for five minutes.'
'I understand that, sir, but I have to tell you that you are not permitted to park your car here and I have to ask you to move it.'
'Five minutes Warden!'
'The time is not the point sir. I have to ask you to move it.'
'Is someone expected or something.'
'Again sir, that is not the point. You are not permitted to park your car . . . '
'I think you are being very unreasonable.'
'I realise that it may sound that way, but I do have to repeat that you are not permitted . . .'

'Fielding' is a technique for taking the sting out of pressure. Listen to what the other person says. Acknowledge that you have heard them using some of the same words and accept that they have a right to their opinion. Accept the truth, however small, in what they say and maintain your position by using the Broken Record technique. You do not have to defend, blame or justify yourself. Stay with the technique. It will be remarkable if one of three things does not happen after about six passes.

1. He moves the car peaceably, with some grumbling at most.
2. He gets unreasonably and impotently angry and moves the car.
3. Some sort of compromise is reached.

'Look, I meant it when I said it was only for five minutes.'
'I realise that, sir. Are you meeting someone.'
'Yes, here at 5 o'clock, they are usually very punctual.'
'Well parking here is not possible, but there is the public parking area. If you care to park there and tell me what the person looks like I will hold the fort until you come back.'

The point of the 'Workable Compromise' is that it can only be reached when you are both being reasonable. The sentence, 'Look, I meant it when I said it was only for five minutes', is the clue that the motorist is no longer treating the Warden as someone he has to beat or be beaten by, but as someone to share a confidence with. They are both talking like human beings – a state we, the authors, believe is the one least likely to end in verbal or physical assault.

A Workable Compromise can only be reached when, and only when, you feel you have resisted the pressure. Listen for clues from the person who is putting you under pressure. Ask yourself what would they reasonably settle for that would not undermine your position: it must work for both of you. Timing is all important: the compromise should not be reached too early nor too late. Remember that Workable Compromises are not always possible.

Dealing with criticism

All of us, including Lone Workers, are inclined to be wrong footed by criticism. Criticism such as: *'You people don't care, you are all the same.' You have no idea what it's like here, you with your safe job.' 'You graduates – you ought to try living out here.'* seem to drive us into justification, blame, unnecessary

WORKING ALONE

explanations and quite often to a counter attack. Unless we are very skilled, criticism brings out the worst in us. It seems to be a way of focusing negative dialogue where the Lone Worker has a *potential attitude problem.*

Table 7.3

Criticism	Attitude triggered by the criticism in the Lone Worker	Faulty internal dialogue – defensive/ passive example	Faulty internal dialogue – combative/ aggressive example
You graduates . . .	Superiority	I'm sorry. My parents were working class	Look, because I have a degree I know best.
You people are just picking on me for little errors that do not really matter.	Perfectionism	I'm sorry but the Ministry insists that everything has to be just so.	Look, if you cannot or won't fill in all the details it will have to go to court.
It's completely unfair. You always bully the little people.	Strength	I'm sorry. But you really ought to be able to pull your socks up.	If you cannot stand up for yourselves, I'm not going to waste any more time with you.
This thing has been going on for years, don't you people realise that.	Urgency	I'm sorry. I'm pretty busy too but I will try to help.	Damn it man, if you showed some sort of urgency at the beginning . . .
Look, haven't you people got enough work to do without . . .	Work ethic	I'm sorry but this is part of my job and I am working 50 hours a week as it is . . .	Who are you to criticise me when you . . .
I never get enough help from you people.	Helping	I'm sorry but we are doing our best.	If you only helped one another instead of criticising me . . .

In Table 7.3 we look at particular criticism that might trigger faulty internal dialogues in Lone Workers. We have given the clusters of faulty internal dialogues names – Elitism, Perfectionism, Strength, Urgency, Work ethic and Help. We are not saying that any of the concepts are *wrong*, but that anyone acting automatically with internal dialogues associated with each of the six is likely to come over as having an *attitude problem*.

Both defensive or aggressive responses are inviting verbal or physical abuse.

We are not saying that professional Lone Workers will actually verbalise the internal dialogues in Table 7.3. We are saying that particular types of criticism will trigger some of our latent attitudes and this will be enough to generate a 'bad' relationship with the client, customer or member of the public. Earlier in the chapter we explained the use of the Broken Record and Fielding techniques to resist pressure, and, indeed, these can be used effectively against all the criticisms we have mentioned in Table 7.3, for instance: 'That's completely unfair. You always bully little people' could be countered by, 'I know it seems like that but fairness is not the issue. The issue is that . . .'.

Our problem is that in the real world, and when we meet a criticism that seems to be aimed directly at us because we do have latent beliefs in the particular area, the reasoned approach of the Broken Record and Fielding techniques is inclined to get lost. The other person is so blatantly attacking the person and not the ball, the trigger to do likewise is virtually automatic. *The clue to our accepting the trigger is a compulsion to say 'Sorry'. When you feel you **have** to reply with the word 'Sorry', then start worrying – they are getting at you.*

We need some way of putting the criticism completely aside before we progress. A useful skill to use is Appropriate Assertion. Whether a valid or invalid criticism from a client, customer or member of the public, either accept it or reject it, whichever is appropriate and *mean* it. Use a firm, level tone and catch the other's eyes. Kill the topic dead – do not allow further discussion – and if possible use some of the other's words in reply. If you find that you are beginning to trust the other person move on to a Constructive Enquiry of what is meant.

'I never get enough help from you people.'
'That is completely untrue. You have been receiving considerable help from us.'

'This thing has been going on for years. Don't you people realise that . . .'
'I accept completely that the thing has been dragging on and for that I apologise.'

'You graduates – you ought to try living here.'
'I accept that I cannot appreciate all the problems of living here.'

The skill of using Appropriate Assertion is that of knowing what you can deny or accept. There are rarely criticisms that do not contain an element of truth and it is important to isolate that element of truth from the global comment. Thus in the first criticism, 'I never get *enough* help from you', the word 'enough' could be the focus of infinite debate. The global criticism needs to be killed and skillfully interpreted. The real issue is that in the other person's view we are not helping adequately and we need to get down to that issue as soon as possible *and without any faulty internal dialogue to fog our professionalism.*

'I never get enough help from you people.'
'That is completely untrue. You have been receiving considerable help from us.'

The very force of denial will have made both the client and the Lone Worker accept a change of direction. Without a change of direction and listening to the faulty internal dialogue, the conversation could have proceeded very badly:

'I never get enough help from you people.'
'You are never satisfied. I've been here virtually every day since Spring.'
'And what have you done. You come here, drink my coffee . . .'

We now have a row with accusations and counter-accusations flying. The Amber sign is moving rapidly to Red. Using Appropriate Assertion, it ceases to be exciting to have a row and we stay on the professional level.

'**That is completely untrue.** You have been receiving considerable help from us.'
'Well it's not enough.'
'*I accept that you feel that way.* What additional help do you need?'
'Well, everything. The children, my husband, the rent, the landlord, the hallway. Have you seen the hallway? Dangerous I call it.'
'**Good. Let me write that lot down. Where shall we start? I have seen the council about the dark area in the hallway . . .**'

Now we are in business. Note the use of the Constructive Enquiry in the last extract to make the most of a valued criticism. When we no longer feel under pressure to blame or justify we can set up a dialogue and learn from a situation. Admit to the element of truth in the criticism and reduce the global criticism to the specific one. Set up priorities, taking one issue at a time, and ask for clarification. Say what is already being done, if relevant, and get their comments on how it affects them and what you can still do to help. Take it slowly: you are the professional and you may well be *starting* the process of getting others to solve their own problems.

Exercise 7.3

Make a list on a notepad of an equal number of totally invalid and valid comments and criticisms made of you, preferably at work. Do not mark the criticisms and comments as to their validity and mix them up. To begin with, attempt to get a colleague to do the same. Swap lists and read the lists to each other.

Use different forms of words, as appropriate. For example, 'That is completely untrue, I am not . . .', (using his or her words) or 'You are absolutely correct, I am . . .', (using their words).

A much more effective way of preparing yourself for a likely problem situation is to use the technique of the Third Position which we discussed in Chapter 6. Empathise with your clients, customers or members of the public, and let yourself 'hear' their likely criticisms. Hear yourself using Appropriate Assertion and Constructive Enquiry and watch from the Third Position. Were you really effective? Did you manage to find the 'ball' rather than the person, and actually assist in the clients' problem-solving process?

It is virtually impossible to foresee every twist but the very process of thinking about things in advance makes it easier to cope with the unexpected. It is not always possible to plan and do things in the ideal way for you, but it is more possible than most of us think.

Criticism properly handled is our window to the world: it is the *'giftie gie us, to see oursels as others see us!'* (Robert Burns).

Constructive Enquiry is the way forward from criticism in the same way as Workable Compromise is the way forward from the buying time techniques of Broken Record and Fielding. The issue of being gentle when using Constructive Enquiry is very important. On the whole few people are used to dealing with people who actually want to communicate.

Giving criticism

Lone Workers often have to criticise others. Just as they may find themselves becoming inadvertently irate because others offer them criticism, other people may feel the same way when they are on the receiving end. Here are some guidelines for constructive feedback.

Practicalities

- Focus on the positive and be seen to be constructive.
- Be clear and explain why *you* are giving the feedback.

- Talk about specifics and things that can be changed.
- Choose the time and place with care – avoid public scenes.
- Plan what you intend to say and close with a summary.
- Remember you have two ears and one mouth – a good counsellor focuses and catalyses but does not originate.
- Don't give advice – listen and assist.

Techniques

- Start on common ground – be clear and take responsibility.
- Watch your own and the other person's body language.
- Meter your own effectiveness.
- Make the ground rules clear – explain what is confidential and what is not.
- Show respect, listen and never ever persecute.

The final issue in this chapter on how the Lone Worker can 'behave themselves into trouble' is about professional distancing – the secret of going home in the evening and living your own life.

Professional Distancing

Lionel is a senior police officer who represents the private and public face of professional concern for his job. About five years ago he arrived at an incident in a rather weather-beaten area in the inner city for which he has responsibility. The homes had seen better days and were inevitably moving from family homes to squats and the bulldozer. One particular house, the scene of aimless vandalism was still owned and occupied by two middle-aged spinster sisters. Lionel charmed the sisters and assisted them personally through the rather distasteful process of identification parades and courtrooms. From then on he received small tributes in the form of cakes and home-made jams from the ladies. They began to appear in his office and finally outside his home on a range of pretexts. At first he was happy to help draft a letter to the council opposing a compulsory purchase order, but it went on. He began to dread going to work and used his wife to check whether the ladies were going to ambush him on his way to the office. Finally he was forced to take out a restraining order on the ladies.

What had happened to Lionel? The two ladies, by skill or accident had forced him to continue a symbiotic relationship where they relied on him and he was trapped. Originally the relationship was appropriate – they did need professional help – but the continuation was not. It had happened in good faith, probably from all three people concerned, but it produced an intolerable situation for Lionel and ended in very bad feelings for everyone.

Many people find themselves being used in some form of symbiosis by others and ultimately what can become a form of slavery makes them have to take drastic action. It may be perfectly OK for you to provide caring support and act as a pair of hands for another, but be aware of what you are doing. A symbiosis is easier to drift into than escape from.

Exercise 7.4

Review the relationships you have in work with your clients, customers and members of the public. Are any of them becoming relationships in their own right with the professional objectives becoming lost?

This chapter has dealt with basic techniques for holding or avoiding dangerous situations. Though obvious and sensible, in practice many of them are not applied. The next chapter deals with the reason for this – we are often not sensible and are our own worst enemies.

8

Stress and anxiety in a conflict situation

Debbie and the cup of coffee too far – What makes events stressful? – Anxiety trait questionnaire – Why it is important to know how we react to potential danger – Perception and appraisal of 'threat' – How to handle anxiety: thought stopping, rethinking, relaxation – Coming to terms with a traumatic incident – Post Traumatic Stress Disorder – Counselling for victims of incidents.

Debbie and the cup of coffee too far

Debbie is a market researcher whose job is to go door to door asking questions about householders' reactions to ranges of products and their promotion on television. She had previously been sent on an 'Assertive Behaviour Course' at the local college and was ready in her own words 'to take the world by storm'. She was a very confident young woman, and happy with her job. She felt that working as she did in a mainly middle-class suburban housing area, she was unlikely to come across many difficult or aggressive people. If people didn't want to speak to her they usually said so and shut the door, and Debbie would just carry on to the next house.

It was a lovely day and Debbie was ahead of time for her quota of respondents. 'The Crescent' was the last road on her list and number 33 was half way down. A young man in his mid-twenties answered the door. He was casually dressed in jeans and a denim shirt but was neat and tidy as he smiled politely:

'*Good afternoon, how can I help you?*'

Debbie produced her card and went into her routine about who she was and the company she was representing and asked if he could spare a few minutes of his time to answer a few simple questions on television advertising. The man agreed, asked her in and offered her a cup of coffee.

Half way through, the man turned to Debbie and asked lightly if she was afraid of going into a strange house with a man she did not know. Debbie began joking about her assertive behaviour training and laughed along with him.

'*You know, you are a very attractive young lady. Why don't you take your shoes off and relax a little. Perhaps, when we have finished the questions, we can get to know each other a little better?*'

Debbie immediately felt uncomfortable and edged away from the man, but he put his hand on her shoulder to prevent her from moving too far away. Debbie froze, she did not know what to say or do. She could not think straight. Her heart began to beat fast and her palms felt hot and sweaty. She could feel herself tensing up and even began to hold her breath.

Suddenly the man let go and chuckled to himself. Debbie took her chance and made for the door which was thankfully unlocked. Leaving her folder and handbag behind her, she ran down the road to the nearest telephone box to call her boss.

Debbie had a lucky escape. Others may not be so lucky. Clearly, what had happened to Debbie had put her under stress and for a moment she was unable to think or act clearly. Later in this chapter we will learn how best to cope when under stress, but for the moment let us concentrate on what happened to Debbie that made her temporarily freeze.

What makes events stressful?

All living things are continuously receiving signals from the outside world. In human beings the neural brain cells make patterns of these signals, and compare all incoming messages, i.e. the signals we receive from our senses, with these patterns. If any of the messages do not fit one of the established patterns the brain sends out an alarm. Thus it is that we can read a book and not be disturbed by the noise of the television, but a large crash sounding from the kitchen is totally unexpected.

This would register as 'foreign' and the brain would cause an alarm to be flashed into the consciousness. In Debbie's case it was the man's remarks about her being attractive which sparked off her alarm.

All our bodies are geared to react very rapidly when what we perceive as danger threatens us. What biologists call the 'fight or flight' mechanism is put into operation. The mechanism prepares the body to cope with any threat or danger by either 'fighting' or 'fleeing'.

The mechanism works by affecting many functions of the body via the *autonomic nervous system*. The pituitary gland releases a biochemical agent, the *adrenocorticotrophic hormone* (ACTH), into the blood stream. Stimulated by ACTH, the adrenal gland secretes adrenalin and other biochemical agents that further arouse and mobilise the body:

- *The senses* become more acute: pupils dilate to improve vision and so spot danger signals; Smell and hearing also become keener. Body awareness is heightened.
- *The heart-rate* increases to pump blood round to supply muscles and allow them to work in either fighting or running away.
- *Blood-flow* is diverted from stomach and kidney to the muscles; this can cause stomach pains (butterflies in the stomach). Blood-flow is lost from the skin resulting in a pale complexion.
- *Clotting time* is reduced to prepare for injury and minimise bleeding.
- *Red blood cells* are produced, thus increasing the transport of oxygen to the muscles.
- *Respiration* is more rapid, increasing the available supply of oxygen.
- *Fat stores* are mobilised to provide energy for muscles, accompanied by an increase in the release of glucose.

H. Selye in *The Stress of Life* (Revised edition, 1956) talks about these bodily reactions that result from exposure to a stressor as the General Adaptation Syndrome (GAS). The GAS consists of three major stages.

- An 'alarm reaction' caused by sudden exposure to a stressful situation. The reaction provides the body with the mechanisms designed to cope with the situation and provides the service of increasing the ability to perform both physically and mentally.
- When exposure to a stressor is prolonged, the alarm mechanism is followed by a stage of 'adaptation' or 'resistance'. The 'adaptation' uses energy which may be needed for other vital functions so it can only function for a limited period.
- The stage of exhaustion.

Debbie was prepared by her body to either run away or resist attack, but feeling that neither was immediately applicable, became anxious and appeared vulnerable. Other people in the same situation could well have appeared angry and aggressive. In either case, the reactions would probably increase the chance of attack for they both involved some loss of control.

The knowledge of stress and anxiety and the practice of relaxation and tension control techniques are vital to the Lone Worker who wishes to deal with problems and remain in control.

But what constitutes a stressful event? Most people would agree that an extreme or life-threatening event would demonstrate stressful characteristics. Most people show a temporary startled reaction to any sudden change in their environment. Whether the stress continues or gets worse depends very much on individual interpretations. An example would be travelling on an underground train or in a lift. For most of us such experiences are part of the daily routine but for someone with claustrophobia, both would be dysfunctionally stressful. Thus, while everyone experiences 'state anxiety' from time to time, there are substantial differences among people in the frequency and intensity with which these states are experienced.

The term *trait anxiety* has been used to describe individual differences in the tendency to see the world as dangerous and in the frequency that state anxiety is experienced over a long period of time. Persons high in trait anxiety (A-Trait) tend to view the world as more dangerous than people with low trait anxiety, and they tend to overreact to their perceptions of threat with more frequent increases in state anxiety. Since high A-Trait people tend to see many different situations as threatening, they are especially vulnerable to stress.

Table 8.1 comprises eight statements which are related to anxiety. Read each statement and ring the number that reflects your present mood. For the questionnaire to be really effective your answer must reflect how you feel *right now*. (Tables 8.1 and 8.2 have been adapted from a recent BBC publication.) *Right now* fits how you feel.

Table 8.1

At this moment in time I feel...	Not at all	Somewhat	Moderately	Very much
...calm.	4	3	2	1
...tense.	4	3	2	1
...upset.	4	3	2	1
...frightened.	4	3	2	1
...nervous.	4	3	2	1
...relaxed.	4	3	2	1
...worried.	4	3	2	1
...confused.	4	3	2	1

Accepting that some of the statements in Table 8.1 may be more related to the clarity of the author's writing than to the reader's state of mind, add up the eight numbers and obtain a total. The set of eight statements in Table 8.2 describe feelings that are related to individual differences in trait anxiety (A-Trait). Again, you should circle the numbers that best fit your present feelings. Add up the eight numbers you have circled to work out your A-Trait scores.

Table 8.2

Under normal circumstances I feel . . .	Almost always	Often	Sometimes	Never
. . . nervous and restless.	4	3	2	1
. . . satisfied with myself and what I have achieved.	4	3	2	1
. . . that things are getting too much for me.	4	3	2	1
. . . like a failure.	4	3	2	1
. . . that I have disturbing thoughts about my contribution.	4	3	2	1
. . . that I lack self confidence.	4	3	2	1
. . . secure.	4	3	2	1
. . . worried over little things.	4	3	2	1

Filling in the questionnaire while you are reading the book will probably leave you with a low – relaxed – anxiety state score on both the questionnaires. Your total score for each questionnaire is likely to be less than 15. Now imagine you have just narrowly missed having a crash in your car. If you filled in the questionnaire truthfully after such an incident you might well get an anxiety state score of between 25 and 30.

In 'stable' conditions the average score for the A-Trait is 15 for males and 16 for females. Individuals who score below 12 are very low in anxiety proneness, and may be somewhat insensitive or unresponsive to other people. Persons with scores of 23 or higher are substantially more anxious than the average person and perhaps unduly sensitive to others. People who are high in A-Trait tend to appraise potentially dangerous situations as more threatening than persons who are low in A-Trait. Readers will find more stress questionnaires at the end of Appendix 3 on stress counselling.

Why it is important to know how we react to potential danger

It is important to know how we react to potential or perceived danger so that we can use the way the body reacts most appropriately. By understanding what our body is doing we can also modify our responses to meet the needs of the moment. In Chapter 2 we discussed stress in terms of remaining in control and it is easier to remain in control if we are prepared, either by prior warning, experience or effective training.

Prior warning, however short, allows us to muster our defences and review our responses. Obviously intense stimuli are more frightening and the soldier about to go into battle can hardly be said to be in control; but even so, the very act of preparing and being prepared is a stabilising factor. Being prepared and having a 'steering wheel' in our hand gives us something to do and potentially makes the stress more manageable. **Experience** also allows us to remain in control and reduces our stress levels. If an event has any predictable features, then even if we may not have a warning as to when it is going to start, but know roughly what will be happening afterwards, we feel more secure. **Effective training** has the effect of allowing us to recognise danger in advance. It increases our awareness of prior warning signals and provides an invaluable exchange of experience.

However well prepared we are, danger and the fear of danger may trigger off the 'fight or flight' mechanism and, if we are alone, our only ally is our own feelings. It is easier to keep control of the situation by listening to our feelings; ignoring feelings can well lose us the security of prior warning. Feelings are a more reliable signal than waiting for the signs of anxiety in others – they may well be watching us!

How we react to a situation depends on our observations, feelings and our appraisal of the level of danger. If the danger is real, we have a chance of taking appropriate action. For example, the pedestrian crossing a busy street may notice a speeding car approaching and will judge the situation to be extremely threatening and take evasive action. If the pedestrian fails to notice the speeding car, the unnoticed danger will not be subjectively appraised as threatening and a serious accident may well be the result. The context in which a potential danger is found will also influence our judgement and actions. The same stimulus may be seen as a threat by one person, a challenge by another, and as largely irrelevant by a third: being made to abseil down a tall building would be seen as a threat to a person with vertigo, a challenge to a person who has never abseiled before and largely irrelevant to an expert.

The experience of 'threat', then, is essentially a state of mind. It has two main characteristics:

- it generally involves the anticipation of a potentially harmful event that has not yet happened; and
- it includes perception, thought, memory and judgement.

Perception and appraisal of 'threat'

We base how we judge the present on what we have seen before.

In Chapter 7 we discussed how our prejudices affect the way we judge other people.

A *Guardian* advertisement on television once showed a young punk rocker pushing a 'respectably' dressed person out of the way on a pavement. The film stopped. The implication was that the punk was assaulting the man. The film started again and the whole scene revealed that the punk had seen that a large object was about to fall on the man and his action of pushing him out of the way had probably saved his life.

The point is well made, but on the whole it is safer to err on the side of caution, continuously updating your analysis of people and situations.

We were once called into a factory which employed a workforce largely composed of young women. The issue was that they were finding that suitable young women seemed to be in embarrassingly short supply. The Personnel Manager, a woman in her late forties, explained the problem:

'They arrive for interview dressed completely unsuitably – dresses well above the knee. I do not know what sort of firm they think it is. Completely unsuitable people for a company founded by Quakers.'

She went on to explain, if explanation was necessary, that anyone who showed her knees was *'no better than she ought to be'*. Unfortunately, the time of the recruitment drive was in the middle of the first era of Mary Quant and the demure women who showed the occasional ankle were in short supply.

If you have had a recent experience which associates a particular style of dress or attitude with danger, it is reasonable to be on your guard when you meet that style of dress or attitude again. Err on the side of safety but be willing to review your attitudes against evidence that you are wrong.

A professional Lone Worker is *not* paid to take risks.

As we have already mentioned, reactions to threats serve an important function when they are based on a realistic appraisal of present or future danger: they can produce emotional arousal that mobilises an individual to take actions to avoid harm. *It is only when our perceptions are inaccurate that we run the risk of worsening the situation.*

Darren is a gentle but large man – someone you wouldn't like to mess with on a dark night. It was the evening after a big match between Manchester United and Leeds and Darren and his friends had been commiserating his team's 3–0 defeat at the hands of Manchester United in the local pub.

On the way home Darren saw two Manchester United fans walking towards him shouting their team's slogans at the top of their voices. On seeing Darren wearing the blue and white colours of Leeds they began hurling abuse about the state of the Leeds' goalkeeper and various other members of the team. Darren perceived the situation as potentially dangerous and his body tensed for either 'fight or flight'.

The remarks made by the other two fans angered Darren to such an extent that he rose to the bait and began hurling abuse back. He found himself in an inappropriately out-numbered 'fight'.

A split lip, a bloody nose and a few bruised ribs later we can see that Darren's perception of the danger and his consequent behaviour made matters worse rather than better.

There are three things Darren could have done to prevent what happened.

1. He could have avoided the danger in the first place by taking a taxi instead of walking.
2. His body was right in sensing potential danger and making the appropriate preparations, however Darren needed to remain in control. The inappropriate internal dialogue that he heard was about aggression: 'They have no right to speak to me in that way. They need showing a lesson. I am bigger than them . . .'. If he had *stopped* and reviewed his internal dialogue he might have heard: 'Yes we lost and they feel pretty good about it. They seem harmless enough, just cocky. Does this necessarily make them a danger? Keep your eyes to yourself, pass by *but be prepared for trouble.*
3. He could have directly reduced the anxiety state itself. We will extend our discussion of this later.

The interpretation of a situation as more or less threatening will depend upon its objective characteristics, the individual's thoughts and memories that are stimulated by the situation, the individual's ability to cope and the person's previous experience with similar circumstances. Objective danger and perception of danger can both equally give rise to an anxiety state therefore it is important to perceive the situation clearly. According to the theory of evolution and natural selection, organisms that either underreact or overreact to dangerous situations are more likely to perish and thus be selected out of the group. Anxiety states are easy to recognise in oneself because they comprise a unique combination of unpleasant feelings and thoughts, as well as the psychological processes we have described above.

How to handle anxiety

The 'fight or flight' response diminishes as the source of stress is removed or resolved but the chemical changes in our bodies may well hang on. So after we have been stressed we must either use up the energy created by it, or learn how to turn off the response using a conscious relaxation exercise or technique. Only then can the body relax again, as the heart rate, blood pressure, oxygen consumption and muscle tension all drop to their normal levels.

Patrick, a teacher, was faced with an extremely angry parent. The parent ranted and raved about issues over which Patrick had no control and on several occasions Patrick thought he was going to be assaulted. Patrick was aware all the time that any form of violent response from him would have made the situation much worse and if he followed his body's fight preparations and his instincts to hit the man, he might well lose his job.

He handled himself well and controlled himself but the body's preparations remained with him. On his return to the staff room one of his colleagues recognised his state, sat him down firmly and made him drink some warm sweet tea. He remained shaking for an hour.

In any stressful situation we have two issues: to avoid the full 'fight or flight' response and to reduce its effect once it is no longer needed. Firstly, we will discuss avoiding the full body response, that is, to *avoid getting so worked up when it is not necessary*.

USING THE 'STOP' SIGN

Patrick certainly made matters worse for himself by his faulty internal dialogue when he encountered the angry parent – phrases like 'it is completely unfair that this man is taking it out on me' and 'what does he know. The child is a complete tearaway and listening to this man, I can understand why'. If he had read Chapter 7 he would have known that he should have blocked out these thoughts and replaced them with 'I accept that I am not the right person to speak to but if I calm him down I may be able to come to the root of the problem'.

It is not as easy, as we may have hinted, to generate the appropriate internal dialogue under the pressure of circumstances. We have already introduced the concept of the Attitude Loop and the use of the STOP sign to pause and review our faulty dialogue. The STOP sign, seen or heard in our mind, interrupts the negative flow of thoughts and allows us to choose appropriate action through positive thinking. The STOP sign may not work for everyone all the time. Readers may find their own way of finding a new direction. We have known people to use such images as the tormentor sitting on a children's potty or allowing the mind to walk through a beautiful garden.

RETHINKING

'Rethinking' is another technique which consists of deliberately letting go of our fears and allowing our emotions to subside as the thoughts go. Imagine you are Debbie at the point at which her internal alarm system has just gone off – she is sensing that the man is about to make a pass. What thoughts are going through your head?

'This is awful. He is going to cause real trouble. There is nothing I can do.'

These are real thoughts and need acknowledging. Listen to them and repeat them to yourself.

Now try repeating the thoughts in your head, or out loud if that is at all appropriate, but without the beginning phrase which implies that you cannot ever be in control.

'Yes, it is a bad situation. All the signs are that I have misread his intentions. I need to regain control and get out.'

Focus your mind on to the reality of the situation and then on to what you are going to do next. Useful conversations to have with yourself at this point may start with:

- What are the facts of the situation?
- What choices do I have at this point?
- What can I do to meet this problem?

The technique is to acknowledge your feelings, stop repeating internal dialogue which fuels your anger or fright, and replace it with rational thought.

RELAXATION

Relaxation can be useful both before the full impact of the body's response mechanism takes hold and to shorten the period of arousal after the incident. Simply telling yourself to relax may well have the opposite effect. As soon as you feel tension of any kind tense up still further and then release completely.

Working with a number of groups of managers in a large company we advocated releasing tension by pressing hard on the underside of a table with the little finger every time they felt stressed. The process transfers the mental pressures of the situation to physical pressures and works very well to aid relaxation.

The apocryphal story was that we trained so many managers in the technique that during a Board meeting where the Senior Executive was being particularly difficult the table rose spontaneously.

Breathing control is a very good method of relaxing. As tension mounts and the alarm mechanism is triggered, you breathe more quickly and more shallowly. In order to ease the tension you need to slow down the rate of breathing and breathe deeply, concentrating on exhaling rather than inhaling. Inhaling often reflects unease of some sort. A sigh of unhappiness, for example, is accompanied by an intake of breath, whereas a sigh of relief is usually an exhalation of air. In situations of extreme difficulty people can even stop breathing temporarily through tension. To stop breathing can be used as a way of dealing with an intense and uncomfortable emotion. Holding yourself together by holding your breath can become a habit.

The technique we would recommend is that of taking six measured breaths – six seconds in, six seconds out, repeated until you feel comfortable. However, it is important to start this exercise by exhaling as this presents hyperventilation.

Severe personal tension is often accompanied by muscle tension. Again we are using the basis of going with the body. If muscles feel tense, make them more tense and then relax them. Developing and using the skill of relaxation needs to be a long-term strategy. When used on a regular basis relaxation will improve your capacity for dealing with stress. Practise the following exercise regularly:

- Let your breath go.
- Take a deep breath and hold it briefly.
- Breathe out slowly and use the sounds 'shoo' or 'hoo'.
- Drop your shoulders.
- Unclench your hands.
- Drop your jaw.
- Purse your lips slightly.
- Count up to ten slowly.
- When you speak do it slowly and in a low tone.

Coming to terms with a traumatic incident

Debbie, our market researcher, managed to escape her difficult situation without coming to any harm, although she was beset by emotional reactions. These would have included fear at what might have happened, anger at the person who caused her fear, relief at her own survival and even some excitement. Any incident which is new and out of the ordinary requires us to pay close attention, and when it involves matters of life and death, it takes a special place in our memory. In Debbie's case, the incident will reverberate in memory so that she can consider every action taken and rehearse the choices she made.

Frightening incidents take an important place in all our everyday memories and only eventually subside when we have understood the implications and checked through all the steps we have taken to deal with it. The memory is never totally lost, only the emotions that surround it become less intense.

But what if Debbie had not been so lucky? Let us assume that Debbie had not managed to escape without harm. How will she then think and rethink about the event? Debbie will still rehearse the actions she took but in a new light – one of failure. She did not judge the situation accurately; she did not react quickly enough; she should not have let herself be taken in by the situation; and perhaps most overwhelming of all, she may ask herself 'Did she lead him on?' In addition to all these judgements there are all the memories and emotions surrounding the attack. The sights and sounds of the incident will bind together actions and consequences in a particular and even painful way.

None of us knows how we would feel if we had undergone a personally frightening incident – at least not until it happens. Success in recovery seems to depend on people's ability to convince themselves that they are blameless, but no one can feel entirely blameless, when they know they could have made other choices. This is the reason why regret and remorse lead to a whole series of 'what ifs'. The emotional consequences of such ordeals are so strong that people will search their memories in order to find ways in which the incident could have been prevented. We may well be using emotions as a learning process – how to deal with the situation better 'next time' – and this may be a painful but useful process. However, unless helped, people often draw conclusions which are not justified and are based on prejudice.

Returning to Debbie, the situation did lead her to review her behaviour constructively. First, she re-evaluated all the specific features which surrounded the attack. That is to say she looked at how she was dressed, the area she worked in, what she said and how she said it. Second, she revised her view of the world. Because of Debbie's experience she now sees the world as a more dangerous place. She will now:

- pay more attention to danger signals;
- be more fearful that the event is going to happen again; and
- pay more attention to her first impressions of her clients.

After traumatic situations we often retain powerful images of the event. These bad memories are powerful enough to generate their own emotional responses. The memories will interrupt people's capacity to do their usual work and make them feel worn out as they go through the detail of the accident again and again. (See below, p. 143). Because of the emotional importance of the event, people undergo a considerable change in their priorities. They withdraw their attention from their usual activities and concentrate more on the memories of the frightening event and begin to make avoidance behaviour. To the outsider they seem preoccupied, unable to think constructively in their normal way, restless in their behaviour and likely to respond with irritability to the usual frustrations of life. Other symptoms to watch for are shown on p. 144. Such is the impact of the event that people may find they have dreams about it and that a lot of their energy is taken up with dealing with emotional consequences of the incident. Because the emotional system has been successful in getting the incident back into the person's mind, they will often feel the need to talk about it, and will do so in a way which is pressured and intense and which may seem surprising and very tiring and unnecessary to others. The casual helpful friend is often inadequate and the professional counsellor essential.

Readers should note that all the reactions we have mentioned are perfectly normal in the immediate aftermath of a traumatic event.

It is usual to lose sleep or appetite or peace of mind when bad things have happened to you. However, it is also usual to begin to adapt and to return to normal after a while. But in the long term the return to normal seems to be the ability to understand what is worth learning about the traumatic event. If one can come to the conclusion which leads to a plan of action then it is easier to resolve one's feelings and to process the emotional material. The whole process now has been given the dramatic name of Post Traumatic Stress Disorder (PTSD). The behaviours associated with PTSD and the symptoms of avoidance behaviour and disordered arousal that victims of traumatic incidents will experience are summarised below. In addition, there is a list of common irrational beliefs of trauma victims.

BEHAVIOURS ASSOCIATED WITH PTSD

Direct responses:

Hyper-vigilance	Intrusive images while awake
Startle reactions	Intrusive thoughts or feelings while awake
Illusions or misperceptions	Re-enactments
Intrusive thoughts or images when when trying to sleep	Rumination or preoccupation
	Difficulty in dispelling thoughts and feelings
Bad dreams	Pangs of emotion
Hallucinations, pseudo-hallucinations	Fears or sensations of losing bodily control

What you do to avoid facing reality:

Inattention, daze	Excessive use of alcohol or drugs
Memory failure	Inhibition of thinking
Loss of train of thought	Unrealistic distortion of meanings
Numbness	Excessive sleeping
Sense of unreality	Avoidance of reminders
Withdrawal	Seeking of distracting stimulation or activity
Misdirection of feelings	

> *What to look for in a person who has had a traumatic experience:*
>
> Hyperactivity
> Retarded pace of actions
> Tremors or tics
> Clumsiness or carelessness
> Autonomic hyper-arousal
>
> Troubled sleep
> Restlessness or agitation
> Exaggerated startle
> Poor concentration
>
> *These are some of the common irrational beliefs following trauma:*
>
> I must never make a mistake.
> I should always be in control.
> I should never ask for help.
> I must never get angry.
> It is weak to show any emotion.
> People in authority are out to get me or must never make a mistake.
> I believe I over-reacted to what happened to me.
>
> The world is a bad and dangerous place.
> I will never get over this.
> I don't care what happens to me.
> No one cares or understands.
> If I don't talk about it things will get better.
> It was all my fault.

Counselling for victims of incidents

The issue of professional counselling is faced by many organisations such as banks and building societies. The Post Office has its own Critical Incident Stress Debriefing Programme. Such a system of early debriefing intervention helps to reduce the possibility of Post Traumatic Stress Disorder.

The aim of trauma counselling is to provide an efficient and effective response to employees who have been the victims of violent attacks. (Violent attacks include all incidents which are perceived as threatening life, liberty or personal security of the employee and which are experienced in the course of their work.) Trauma counselling provides a simple support system which is easily understood by both management and employees. The system incorporates a case-monitoring element which enables a benefits analysis to be undertaken. The benefits for the manager are improved skills and professionalism in managing employees who have been involved in violent incidents. They also have clear guidelines on the referral of employees for further help. The employee benefits from immediate help and support in dealing with the feelings and emotional upset of being involved in a violent incident, thereby reducing the likelihood of long-term stress problems. They are also given practical advice and information. The organisation which implements a trauma counselling service gains an enhanced image as one which cares about the safety and welfare of its employees. There is also a reduction in employee illness resulting from violent incidents. But most importantly, *the emotional needs of victims of a traumatic incident are recognised and addressed* by management, the Operational Health Service and welfare services. Where the need is recognised, a programme of debriefing should be considered both on a formal or an *ad hoc* basis.

SETTING UP A CRITICAL INCIDENT STRESS DEBRIEFING PROGRAMME

If your organisation is thinking about setting up a Critical Incident Stress Debriefing Programme, there are several factors that need to be considered.

1. Establish the need in your organisation.
2. Decide if your organisation can share resources with one or more organisations interested in the same type of services.
3. Seek out psychological or social work professionals who are willing to work with you.
4. Determine if the services might be offered free of charge. If costs are going to be involved, how much?
5. The following are the usual sources of psycho-social support professionals:

    - hospital social work departments;
    - universities and colleges with psychology or social work departments;
    - community mental health centres;
    - crisis counselling centres;
    - private psychologists, social workers, psychiatrists;
    - psychiatric nurses, mental health counsellors;

- priests, ministers, rabbis; and
- mental hospitals.

Once the early decisions have been made and professional help enlisted, a management team can begin to put a system into practice. The Occupational Health Executive also offers valuable advice. An outline of its recommended debriefing programme can be found in Appendix 3 and organisations wishing to implement a victim support service should follow the OHE's model.

Factors which help a personal return to stability after a traumatic incident

The most important factor in assisting a victim to return to stability seems to be to get the sufferer to confront the disturbing material and to pay attention to it. Stimuli which were associated with the traumatic event should be looked at and experienced again by the sufferer. In order not to upset the person unnecessarily, a safe setting must be created, and the victim must trust the skills of the professional therapist. The safe place must be one where the person can show emotions and fear freely, knowing that he/she will have support and the time to go through the presentation of the disturbing material until he/she is able to feel calm again. Such debriefing gets the victim used to the sights, sounds and smells of his/her experience until he/she can experience it without upset and making the traumatic link between a particular stimulus and the emotion of fear.

The other factor which helps in the debriefing process is the use of therapy sessions. Again these must be conducted in safety where he/she can calmly rehearse his/her actions, especially concentrating on how he/she coped with the situation. By paying attention to what the person did to control the situation the therapist can begin to increase the victim's sense of mastery and make it easier for him/her to process the event. It is important to get the right balance between exposing the person to traumatic stimuli and maintaining his/her sense of control and mastery.

Factors that hinder a personal return to stability after a traumatic incident

If no confrontation with the distressing stimuli of the event takes place then the link between the stimuli and the fear remains unbroken. Indeed, because the memory makes people even more frightened, there is every possibility that the fear will get greater and greater. Above all, the successful treatment of a person who has undergone a traumatic event depends upon the ability to assist that person to confront his/her fears with a sense of control, relaxation and mastery.

The role of the manager after traumatic incidents

The individual line manager responsible for the worker who has been involved in a particular incident may or may not be the best person for the debriefing we recommend and which is included in Appendix 3. The overall role of the manager is to understand, direct appropriate help for the individual and to learn from the experience so that it may be avoided in future. Information from the debriefing should be fed into the incident reporting procedures we detailed in Chapter 3. Incidents of verbal and physical abuse are serious to organisations but most of all they are serious to individuals. As we said in the beginning of the book, they are both more common and more serious for the Lone Worker.

9

The great debates – drawing the line somewhere

Should we be trained in self-defence techniques – Equality?

It is impossible to venture into the world of Lone Workers and their personal security without being dragged into two debates. The first debate is on whether self-defence training is a good thing or not; the second is about equality. The equality debate is far the most complex because it involves the whole range of emotions and raises issues about fundamental value systems. We will discuss the issue of self-defence first. Obviously, it is preferable for the Lone-Worker to think in terms of 'self-protection' rather than self-defence and to try to avoid getting into situations that require defence. However, self-defence is a subject worth giving thought to.

Should we be trained in self-defence techniques?[1]

Before we begin it is sensible to define terms. Virtually everything we have discussed up until now is 'self-defence' in some form or another. Here we are discussing self-defence in its physical manifestations, for example Judo, Karate, etc., given in formal instruction to Lone Workers with a view to increasing their self-confidence and allowing them to repel violent attack.

---

[1] A further set of issues arise should individuals or organisations take up training for self-defence. These issues are concerned with insurance and claims civil and perhaps criminal can arise should 'skilled' people inflict actual bodily harm.

Up until very recently self-defence training was seen as a 'good thing' and is, if correctly taught, effective in certain critical situations. It also has advantages for the individuals concerned, providing an enjoyable sociable event which not only teaches the practical aspects of self-defence but also increases confidence and raises awareness. The acceptance of a training programme also acts as a motivating factor for individuals who feel that their needs are being accepted and understood.

But self-defence training does now have an increasing band of critics. First, it can lead to over-confidence, especially if training is not repeated at regular and frequent intervals. People who have been trained in self-defence techniques may assume that 'fighting' may be the best resort in tricky situations but this assumes that the Lone Worker will 'win'. In reality very few of us have the benefit of the choreographer working with Bruce Lee. We may well be outnumbered, smaller or even be facing a better trained athlete than ourselves. Violence very often begets violence.

Second, self-defence can often be the wrong response to a potentially violent incident. If employees are thinking about ways to defend themselves, they are less likely to be listening to what their potential assailant has to say. Instead, they should be looking for ways to calm them down and to resolve the situation peacefully.

In all cases, self-defence, even if used 'successfully', will be a second-best option. Ideally, violence is to be avoided and no injury caused to either party. The police also express considerable reservations about widespread self-defence training for the general run of employees. Staff themselves are often reluctant to be trained in self-defence, taking the not unreasonable view that by providing training, management is accepting that there may be some circumstances in which self-defence will have to be used.

Equality?

There is no simple or easy way to discuss the issues on equality brought up by the problems that made this book necessary.

We were working with a mixed group of Lone Workers developing safety procedures. As the issues unfolded the sexes separated out. Several of the men adopted extreme attitudes: *'Well if **they** cannot do the job . . .'*, *'If it costs more then **they** should get paid less'*; and the women naturally got defensive. To us, it seemed that elements in the organisation, hopefully a minority, were using the safety debate as a stalking horse for deeper male prejudice.

The attitudes that came to light in such an ugly way in this incident are not, in our experience, unusual and because they often seem to be near the surface in any debate, make logical analysis difficult. Let us put our cards on the table.

- We regard certain jobs as intrinsically dangerous.
- We regard it as a moral, as well as a legal, obligation of staff and employers to reduce the risks on these jobs to an acceptable level.
- We accept that the reduction of risk to an acceptable level may mean major revision and possible losses of some jobs.
- We accept that 'acceptable level' is a grey area, part of which lies in public debate and is subject to Risk Assessment, but part is also based on the judgement of the individual Lone Worker. If an individual Lone Worker judges a particular part of his or her work is unacceptably dangerous *for him/her*, this view should be respected.
- We accept that the 'intrinsic risk' of some jobs may be increased from acceptable to unacceptable levels by the characteristics of the individual workers involved. We do not accept that the crude split of male/female is the only or, indeed, ever a guide to decisions on employment. For us, the emphasis is on the word INDIVIDUAL. Taking the argument to absurdity, it would be ridiculous to employ a partially sighted person to direct traffic. It is probable that

procedures and technology could be developed to allow him or her to do the job, but we have to ask why and what would we be trying to prove. At less absurd levels, colour, physical disability, sexual orientation, physical size and demeanour, religious grouping, class, age, etc., might *all* be seen in particular situations to make individuals work at higher intrinsic risk than their fellows.

- Where intrinsic safety is an issue and the job needs to be done, one solution would be redeployment of individuals in the organisation so that people with suitable qualifications could do the right job. In principle, and we accept the danger of using such a word, an individual should not be thought of, or treated, unfavourably because of such redeployment.

- We accept that the ideal solution is unlikely, even in large organisations; in small organisations it could be virtually impossible. The solution, as we see it, would be based on a sensible recruitment policy and a realistic analysis of the jobs in all organisations. The recruitment policy must be based on analysis and not on prejudice. What we are saying here could be taken, by those who wish to hear it that way, as discrimination, but we would emphasise our words *realistic analysis*. At the extreme, we would not hire a partially sighted person as a traffic controller or, indeed, a sixty-year-old as a postal worker on deliveries. *The problem is where to draw the line*.

- As a final point we would question the many sources of training materials. In our view they emphasise the 'defenceless woman' role. We would single out for criticism a film produced by the Rover Group in conjunction with the Metropolitan Police. Again in our view, the message of this film is that all men are beasts and that women *need* to be protected in a harsh world.

In writing this book we have become increasingly aware that the world is becoming less forgiving and more hostile. We are also aware that more and more of us are being forced into the role of the Lone Worker.

Together these two trends will mean more headlines, more heartache and more personal tragedy. The pressure is on those of us who are lone workers to be aware and limit our risk to personally acceptable levels.

The pressure on those of us who manage lone workers is again awareness, but this time focused by very strong legislative pressure.

Appendix 1

An example of a violent incident report form

■

Date of incident   Day of week   Time

EMPLOYEE – Personal details of person assaulted

NAME _____

SEX _____ ETHNIC CATEGORY _____

JOB TITLE _____ DEPARTMENT _____

HOME ADDRESS _____

Details of the Assailant (if known)

NAME _____

ADDRESS _____

AGE (approx) _____ SEX _____

PLEASE GIVE DESCRIPTION _____

WHO WAS THE OTHER PARTY TO THE INCIDENT? (Delete as appropriate)
Client/Member of the public/Don't know

WERE THERE ANY WITNESSES TO THE INCIDENT?

No ☐   Yes ☐

If yes, please state who: _____

Details of the incident

WHERE DID THE INCIDENT HAPPEN?_____

Please tick the relevant box to indicate the type of violent incident you were involved in:

- ☐ Physical Assault
- ☐ Sexual Assault
- ☐ Harassment of worker with disability
- ☐ Abuse of worker with disability
- ☐ Assault of worker with disability
- ☐ Threat or fear of one of these
- ☐ Sexual Abuse
- ☐ Racial Abuse
- ☐ Verbal Abuse
- ☐ Racial Harassment
- ☐ Sexual Harassment

State which: _____

WHAT HAPPENED?
(Please include background to the incident)

DID YOU RECEIVE ANY INJURIES?   No ☐   Yes ☐

If yes, please give details: _____

REGARDLESS OF WHETHER YOU RECEIVED ANY INJURIES OR NOT, DID YOU SEEK MEDICAL HELP?

No ☐   Yes ☐

If yes, please state where:
Name and address (if known) _____

DID YOU LEAVE WORK IMMEDIATELY AFTER THE INCIDENT?

No ☐   Yes ☐

ARE YOU OFF WORK DUE TO THE INCIDENT?

No ☐   Yes ☐

DID YOU RETURN TO WORK IMMEDIATELY AFTER THE INCIDENT?

No ☐   Yes ☐

WERE YOU THE ONLY EMPLOYEE INVOLVED IN THE INCIDENT?

No ☐   Yes ☐

If no, please state who else was involved: _____

DID ANYONE ELSE RECEIVE INJURIES?

No ☐   Yes ☐

If yes, please state who: _____

WAS MONEY INVOLVED?

No ☐   Yes ☐

If yes, who's? _____

WERE THE POLICE INVOLVED?

No ☐   Yes ☐

If yes, give police details: _____

WERE ANY STATEMENTS MADE TO THE POLICE?

No ☐   Yes ☐

Other information

POSSIBLE CONTRIBUTORY FACTORS

IS THE ASSAILANT KNOWN TO HAVE BEEN INVOLVED IN ANY PREVIOUS INCIDENTS?

No ☐   Yes ☐

If yes, please state: _____

DO YOU ENVISAGE FURTHER ACTION BEING TAKEN WITH REGARD TO THE INCIDENT?

No ☐   Yes ☐

IF PREVENTATIVE MEASURES HAVE BEEN IDENTIFIED WHAT STEPS HAVE BEEN TAKEN TO INFORM THE RELEVANT PEOPLE?

ANY OTHER RELEVANT INFORMATION

Appendix 2
Safety guidelines for Lone Workers

■

The following guidelines have been adapted from 'A *Guide to Safe Travel*' published by the Suzy Lamplugh Trust.

Identification Cards

- Always show your identification card (or business card) or wear it in a prominent position.
- Do not allow it out of your possession.
- Give the client time to study the ID card.

Check for obvious dangers, for example dogs, hazard signs, etc.

If you enter premises

- Park your vehicle in a safe and obvious place, leaving yourself a quick escape route.
- Always lock your vehicle.
- Only enter when invited and if safe to do so.

Yourself and your environment

- Remember no one is invincible – it is folly to think it will never happen to you.
- Trust your feelings. If you feel uneasy or scared do not ignore the warnings. Act on your intuition.

Be alert

- Walk tall: good posture and balance are positive aids to self-protection and also give you an air of self-assurance.
- Keep your mind focused on your surroundings – be aware of your environment.

Avoid putting yourself at risk

- Do not give your home telephone number or your address to clients.

- Avoid after-hours appointments.
- Do not get into a lift with anyone who makes you feel uneasy.
- Wear clothes which give out the signals you intend. We may not all want to conform to the expected professional image but we need to be aware of the effect we create.

TRAVEL

Prepare yourself for the journey

- Plan your route (know where you are going and how you are going to get there).
- Tell someone where you are going.
- Watch what you wear.
- If travelling in your own car, make sure it is well-maintained and that you have enough petrol for your journey.

Avoid risks

- Decline offers from strangers.
- Keep to familiar roads.
- Avoid spur of the moment changes *en route*.

Never even think:

- *It won't happen to me.*
- *I can cope.*
- *It's only a short journey.*
- *They look OK.* Try not to judge people from their appearance.

On foot

- Place valuables such as wallets in an inside pocket.
- Avoid deserted places, dark buildings, bushes, waste ground, car parks and alleyways.
- Be alert at subways, take advantage of other people going your way.
- If you need to go through a 'risk' area, think about what you would do if faced by a problem. Look for escape routes. Walk in the middle of the pavement; don't walk too close to doorways.
- If you do think you are being followed, trust your instincts and take action.

As confidently as you can, cross the road, turning as you do to see if someone is behind you. If they cross to you, re-cross again and again, keep moving. If he continues to follow, make for a busy area – a pub, service station or other public premises. Go in and telephone the police and a friend. Also tell the manager, or a cashier or anyone else who is likely to help you. Try not to speed up if you think someone is following you. This is a clear indication that you have noticed him and that you are worried by it. Instead, purposely slow down. If the person behind slows down too you can be quite sure that he is following you but at the same time you will not let him know that you are aware of his presence. This will buy you more time to clear your thoughts and to plan what you are going to do.

- If a vehicle pulls up suddenly alongside you, turn and walk in the other direction – you can turn much faster than a car.
- Never accept a lift from a stranger.
- Beware of a stranger who warns you of the danger of walking alone and then offers to accompany you. This is a ploy some attackers have been known to use.

By car

When in your car, you are safer in some ways but more vulnerable in others.

- Stay in the car as much as possible, keep the windows closed. Keep the doors locked, if you feel safer this way. Some people prefer not to lock the driver's door in case of an accident.
- Keep bags out of sight.
- Keep your car in good working order and carry extra petrol in a special safety-approved petrol can.
- If you own a car, it is advisable to be a member of one of the breakdown organisations.
- Keep a map handy so you won't need to stop and ask directions.
- Have change or a phone card for a pay-phone in an emergency.
- A great asset is a car phone. They are expensive but worth it.
- At night park in a well-lit place. When you get back, check the back seat. Have a pocket torch handy and your keys in your hand, ready for a quick getaway.

- If you park in daylight, consider what the area will be like in the dark.
- If you are followed to your car and confronted, throw your bag or briefcase to the ground. If that person intends to rob you he might just pick up the bag and go, leaving you alone. This action will also have the effect of startling him thereby giving you just a couple of seconds to gather your thoughts.

Regular car maintenance is essential.

- Read your car maintenance manual and stick to the routine procedures for weekly and monthly maintenance.
- Regular servicing will keep your car in good mechanical order but minor problems can still occur. Don't turn a blind eye in the hope that faults will disappear. Get into the habit of carrying out routine checks on your car.
- Ensure that you always have enough petrol or diesel. (In 1991 the AA recorded 33,000 instances of drivers running out of fuel.)
- Carry an emergency car kit.
- Join a motoring organisation.

Motorways

Travel on motorways is becoming an increasing concern, especially when a breakdown occurs or assistance is needed. Opinions are divided as to what to do or what not to do. Use your judgement according to the circumstances.

- Drive to an emergency telephone if you can, stopping with the front passenger door as close to the telephone as possible.
- Switch on your hazard lights; if leaving the vehicle do so by the nearside door.
- Never cross the carriageway to reach a closer telephone.
- If you cannot drive further, a marker post (every 100 metres) will point to the nearest telephone which are set 1000 metres apart. You will never need to walk further than 500 metres.
- No money is required. As soon as you lift the handset, it will start ringing in the Police control room. You need not say where you are; they will know.

- Stand behind the telephone and watch out for traffic and anyone approaching you. The passing traffic makes it very noisy; you may have to shout.
- Tell the control if you are a woman on your own. They will alert a police car to check that you are all right.
- If you are by the telephone and someone stops, use the telephone to tell the police, giving them the registration number of the car that has stopped.
- If your car is not near the telephone, note the numbers on the nearest marker post. Tell the control room the problem and have your breakdown organisation card and your car registration number ready.
- The Highway Code advises you to decide whether or not to stay in the car or stand on the verge. The Department of Transport, Police, RAC and AA's advice is to stay on the verge, only re-entering the car if you feel in danger. Ten per cent of all fatal motorway accidents take place by a vehicle colliding with a car on the hard shoulder. Try to decide by considering all the factors: the weather, the time of day and whether it is dark and deserted, or busy and well lit.
- If you decide to stay on the verge, do not leave the keys in the car; lock all the car doors except the passenger door which you should leave fully open so that you can get back in quickly if you decide to. Then lock the passenger door behind you.
- When the breakdown truck arrives, check that he knows your name and that he has in fact been sent to you. Some breakdown trucks cruise, waiting to pirate custom.
- Police in some areas have found that a notice stating, 'Help – Phone the Police' placed in the back window of the car has been successful.

Taxi and Mini Cabs

Mini cabs or private hire vehicles are unlicensed. Mini-cab drivers are not vetted so it is advisable that you follow these guidelines.

Outside London, recent legislation has tightened up the law and now in most districts the private hire cars are licensed and the drivers carefully checked.

- Make sure you have the telephone number of a reputable car company. Ask your friends for a recommendation.
- When booking your cab you must do so by telephone. Ask the company for the driver's name and even the call sign. Ask what type of car it is.
- If you are calling from a public place, try to avoid doing so where someone overhears you giving your name, etc. Anyone could pull up and call 'cab for Mary Smith', so when your cab arrives, check the driver's name and company.
- While you may not wish to appear unfriendly, always sit in the back.
- If you do talk to the driver, don't give any personal details.
- If you feel uneasy with the driver, ask him to stop at a busy familiar place and get out.
- Before arriving at your destination have your money ready, leave the cab and then pay the driver.
- *Beware of bogus mini-cabs.*
  Some people falsely represent themselves as mini-cab (in London; outside London as private hire car) drivers, with aerials on their car roofs and pretend handsets. They unlawfully ply for hire at busy night spots, gaining fares by calling out, 'Someone ordered a cab?'.

Travelling on public transport

Public transport is generally safe. The fear of attack on bus or train is far greater than the reality. Below are guidelines taken from the booklet *'Travel Safely by Public Transport'*, compiled by the Suzy Lamplugh Trust and the Department of Transport with the co-operation of London Underground Ltd., The Bus and Coach Council, British Rail and the British Transport Police.

Safety Tips

- Plan ahead. Have the right change for your fare so that you do not have to fumble in your wallet or bag.
- If you buy a ticket from an office, put your change/card/cheque book away safely before leaving the till.
- Consider buying a season ticket – you'll need to find your money less often.

- When getting off a bus or train at night, attach yourself to groups of people also leaving. Or arrange a friend or a taxi to meet you.
- Know where you are going and which stop you need. If you look at a map it shows that you don't know the area and may leave you open to dubious offers of help.
- Carry a personal alarm and know how to use it.
- When waiting for a bus at night, stand in a well-lit place near groups of people.
- On the bus sit near the driver and choose an aisle seat. On a double-decker bus the lower deck is preferable.
- If there is an incident on a bus, make a fuss straight away. The driver can alert the Police or Head Office if he has a radio.

On trains

- Avoid travelling in compartments with no access to corridors and other parts of the train. These are being phased out but there are still a few left.
- Don't be afraid to pull the communication cord or alarm. No one will blame you for a genuine mistake.
- Don't hesitate to alert the guard, conductor or any railway official if you feel threatened by a fellow passenger. The staff will then keep a special eye open for you and alert the Police if necessary.

The British Transport Police

The British Transport Police are the national police for Britain's railways including the London Underground. Whether you are the victim of a crime or need assistance or advice, they will help you efficiently and sympathetically.

They can be contacted through the many offices at main stations, through Help Points on Underground stations, through rail staff, through any police station or you can call them directly on 071-380 1400 or by dialling 999.

Appendix 3
Stress counselling

■

MANAGER GROUP DISCUSSIONS/DEBRIEFING AFTER A TRAUMATIC INCIDENT

The purpose of the debriefing session is to enable the victim to talk about his/her feelings of distress. To do this soon after the violent event prevents development of long-term problems. It is vital that management takes its full role because the whole system depends upon managers fulfilling the link between the victim and the help which is available. The role of the manager is to:

(a) facilitate the debriefing process;
(b) identify particularly vulnerable individuals;
(c) explain the various options of help that are available, inform the victim's general practitioner of the incident and arrange an appointment with the Operational Health Service (OHS) or welfare services as necessary; and
(d) watch for symptoms of stress in following months.

(a) The debriefing process

During violent incidents it is normal for people to feel vulnerable, helpless and powerless to resist. Afterwards there may be feelings of anger, guilt and fear of another attack. These feelings take time to work through. Distressed people should be encouraged to talk openly about their experiences, what happened, what they did and how they felt.

Individual coping skills vary. The purpose of the debriefing process is to build on the individual's own effective coping ability and to identify people who may be adopting inappropriate or damaging 'coping' methods.

The initial Manager/Victim Debriefing Session must be timed as close to the traumatic event as possible, preferably on day 1 or 2. The place of the meeting is important – it should be comfortable, provide refreshments, allow for no interruptions, and be private and confidential. Make arrangements to have a room available for the debriefing session. Allow about one and a half hours for the meeting.

The main skills required for the debriefing process are:

- active listening
- appropriate responding
    - open questions
    - paraphrasing
    - summarising
- empathy
    - body language
    - understanding

(b) Identification of vulnerable individuals

Some people are more vulnerable to post-traumatic distress than others. The manager should take particular care with people who:

- were involved as a hostage, particularly in their own home;
- have had emotional problems in the past, e.g. depression, sleeping difficulties, stress, etc;
- are loners and who find it difficult to talk about themselves or their feelings;
- have experienced an earlier violent event;
- live alone; and
- feel responsible for others.

Where the manager feels that an individual needs additional help or counselling this should be identified in any records. Debriefing training will also help you to identify individuals who may require further help.

(c) Arrange an appointment with OHS or welfare services

When people are shocked and upset they find it very difficult to concentrate. It is important, therefore, that they are told how they can get help.

Any violent incident can leave the victim feeling isolated, shocked, and thinking 'why me?' Talking over what happened with someone who cares, can help the victim to come to terms with the experience and help to prevent long term-distress. *It is quite normal to feel shaken-up by a violent attack.*

The victim may feel:

- angry
- anxious
- unable to concentrate
- emotional
- numb
- tearful
- irritable
- jumpy
- tired
- unable to sleep
- gulity
- tense
- isolated
- restless
- depressed
- alone

All these feelings are normal and should begin to fade within a week or so. Sometimes the feelings do not go away, perhaps they start at a later date. Her are some useful hints – some dos and don'ts – for dealing with the feelings:

DO

- talk about your feelings;
- ask for help;
- speak to your GP;
- try relaxation or physical exercises to unwind; and
- go back to the workplace.

DO NOT

- drink alcohol;
- take unprescribed sleeping pills or other medication;
- cut yourself off from your workplace;
- get overtired;
- skip meals; or
- bottle things up.

Where an individual has been identified as needing additional support or counselling the local Occupational Health Service or Welfare Department can be contacted. The decision on where the victim should be referred is dependent upon needs of the actual case.

(d) Watch out for delayed symptoms

Sometimes someone may have appeared to have handled a traumatic situation well and be back to normal almost immediately. Then quite out of the blue something happens and the individual begins to show delayed symptoms of shock. The individual's manager will need to be sensitive to the unexplained changes in the employee's performance, behaviour or emotions, and if such changes do occur, to point out that he/she is concerned about the employee's performance and to suggest that he/she may wish to seek counselling from OHS. The following are common symptoms of delayed stress:

- poor performance
  - missed deadlines
  - lack of concentration
- minor accidents
- anger
- irritability
- depression
- loss of interest
- lateness
- increase in sickness absence
- any symptoms of changed behaviour.

If this is the case then often the victims are asked to fill in the following Stress Assessment Questionnaires.

THE USE OF STRESS ASSESSMENT QUESTIONNAIRES

Stress Assessment Questionnaires are produced by the Occupational Health Service and should be used some months after the incident, although, if it is thought to be necessary, they could be given after a fortnight has elapsed. They should be given primarily to those who do not appear to have recovered from the effects of the incident.

The questionnaires are intended to be given to people to complete on their own. However, it is often better to help those who might otherwise not be able or willing to write down their answers by going through it with them. There are two questionnaires which make up this assessment. The first, The Impact of Events Questionnaire, asks questions about the incident and its effects. The second questionnaire looks at your general health.

THE IMPACT OF EVENTS QUESTIONNAIRE

Below is a list of comments made by people after a stressful event. Please check each item and indicate how frequently these comments were true for you *during the past seven days*. If they did not occur at all, tick the 'Never' box.

Comments — Frequency: Never, Rarely, Sometimes, Often

1. I thought about it when I did not mean to.
2. I avoided letting myself get upset when I thought about it or was reminded of it.
3. I tried to remove it from my memory.
4. I had trouble falling or staying asleep because of pictures or thoughts of it coming into my head.
5. I had waves of strong feelings about it.
6. I had dreams about it.
7. I stayed away from reminders of it.
8. I felt as if it had not happened or it was not real.
9. I tried not to talk about it.
10. Pictures of it popped up into my mind.
11. Other things kept making me think of it.
12. I was aware I still had lots of feelings about it, but did not deal with them.
13. I tried not to think about it.
14. Any reminders brought back feelings about it.
15. My feelings about it are numb.

Scoring
Only items 1 to 15 are added up to get the final total. Any answer in the 'Rarely' category gets a score of one, 'Sometimes' gets a score of three; The 'Often' category gets a score of five. As a rule of thumb, any score of 15 or over is indicative of problems, and any score of 30 or more certainly indicates problems.

GENERAL HEALTH QUESTIONNAIRE

We would like to know if you have had any medical complaints, and how your health has been in general over the past *few weeks*. Please answer all the questions by ticking the box which most nearly applied to you.

Have you recently — Never   Rarely   Sometimes   Often

1. Felt unwell and in poor health?
2. Felt in need of a good tonic?
3. Felt run down and out of sorts?
4. Felt you are ill?
5. Been getting pains in the head?
6. Been getting a feeling of tightness or pressure in your head?
7. Had hot and cold spells?
8. Lost a lot of sleep through worry?
9. Had difficulty in staying asleep?
10. Felt constantly under strain?
11. Got edgy or bad tempered?
12. Got scared or panicky for no reason?
13. Found everything getting on top of you?
14. Felt nervous and strung-up?
15. Kept yourself busy?
16. Been able to get things done?
17. Felt on the whole you were doing things well?
18. Felt satisfied with the ways you have done things?
19. Felt you were playing a worthwhile part in things?
20. Felt capable of making decisions about things?
21. Been able to enjoy your normal daily activities?
22. Felt yourself to be a worthless person?
23. Felt life is entirely hopeless?
24. Felt life is not worth living?
24. Thought that you might do away with yourself?
26. Felt you could not do anything because your nerves were too bad?
27. Found yourself wishing you were dead and out of it?
28. Found the idea that taking your life kept coming to your head?

Scoring

This questionnaire is marked by giving any answer to the right of the midpoint a score of 1, and any answer to the left of the midpoint a score of 0. The scores are then simply added up to get the final total. If you want you can also look at the sub-scores.

The first 7 items cover the Somatic Complaints scale; 8–14 cover the Anxiety scale; 15–21 the Social Dysfunction scale; and 22–28 the Severe Depression scale. Total scores of 4 and below on the whole scale can be ignored. Scores in the 5 to 12 range suggest problems; scores of 13 to 20 even more so; and scores above 20 certainly require attention.

Appendix 4

Assessing stress and the Lone Worker

∎

The following questions are designed to help you pin-point the areas of your work where stress is occurring.

Your job

- Do you feel put-upon or feel you are working too hard?
- Do you regularly work during lunchtimes or evenings?
- Do you never have holidays?
- Are you depressed by your working environment?
- Do you find it difficult to cope with a recent promotion?
- Do you feel unable to ask your boss for a rise or a holiday?
- Do you feel bored with your job?
- Do you find it difficult to organise your work, or are you required to do too many different things at once?
- Do you think that communication channels are very poor at your place of work?
- Does your job involve the pressure of constant deadlines?
- Do you find that constant interruptions ruin your concentration?
- Do you feel your talents and abilities are not fully recognised?
- Do you have to work at relentless, mechanical tasks without the chance to rest?

Your management of time

- Do you usually try to do things as quickly as possible?
- Do you run out of time when working on important projects?
- Do you deliberately try to do several things at once?

- Do you regularly forget about appointments or important deadlines?
- Do you rarely plan any of your activities more than a day or two in advance?
- Do you talk and walk quickly?
- Do you get impatient easily?
- Do you always feel in a hurry?
- Do you feel that time is passing by too quickly?
- Does time spent travelling get you down?
- Do you always travel to work in the rush hour?
- Does your partner get annoyed because you spend too much time working?
- Do you only rarely give yourself a break to play, relax, laze or dream?
- Do you feel you spend too much time at home with the children?
- Do you spend the majority of your time with other people, with little time on your own?
- Do you often lose your temper because there never seems to be enough time to finish what you need to do?
- Do you never use a diary?

If the answer to the majority of these questions is yes, then you could be prone to stress.

Appendix 5

The Health and Safety regulations in force from January 1993

■

The new regulations are needed to implement six European Community (EC) Directives. They cover:

- Health and Safety Management
- Work Equipment Safety
- Manual Handling of Loads
- Workplace Conditions
- Personal Protection Equipment
- Display Screen Equipment

An additional Directive relating to work on construction sites is also relevant.

The new regulations are enforceable although formal enforcement is not likely unless:

- the risks to health and safety are evident and immediate;
- what needs to be done is not new (i.e. existing duties transposed into new legislation);
- employers appear deliberately obdurate and unwilling to recognise their responsibilities to ensure the long-term health, safety and welfare of employees and others affected by their activities.

The new regulations are of vital concern to Lone Workers and their employees and this summary based on a Health and Safety Executive leaflet should not be taken as more than an introduction. We will detail the proposals of the first regulation – Management of Health and Safety Regulations at Work Regulations 1992 – as being the most relevant.

APPENDIX 5

The regulations will require you to:

- assess risks for putting into practice the health and safety of your employees and of anyone else who may be affected by your work activity. This is so that the necessary preventative and protective measures can be identified. Employers with five or more employees will have to record the significant findings of the assessment. (The same threshold is already used in the Health and Safety at Work Act. Employers with five or more employees will have to record their arrangements;
- provide appropriate health surveillance for employees where the risk assessment shows it to be necessary;
- appoint competent people (either from inside your organisation or from outside) to help you devise and apply the measures you need to take to comply with your duties under health and safety law;
- set up emergency procedures;
- provide your employees with information they can understand about health and safety matters;
- co-operate with other employers sharing your work site;
- make sure that your employees have adequate health and safety training and are capable enough at their jobs to avoid risks; and
- provide temporary workers with some particular health and safety information to meet special needs.

The regulations will also:

- place duties on employees to follow health and safety instructions and report danger; and
- extend the current law which requires you to consult employees' safety representatives and provide facilities for them.

These general duties will lie side-by-side with the more specific ones in other health and safety regulations. But that does not mean that you have to do things twice. For example, if you have done a risk assessment to comply with the COSHH (Control of substances hazardous to health) Regulations you will not have to do it again for the same hazardous substances to comply with the management regulations. A specific duty will normally take the place of a general one that duplicates it.

We give below an example of a Risk Assessment form which we have completed using Pools collectors as a model. The columns 'Likelihood of occurrence' and 'Severity of hazard' are rated on a scale of 1–5, 5 being the greatest. The 'Seriousness' in the next column is the product of these two and indicates the priority of treatment.

Risk Assessment form completed using Pools collectors as a model

Hazards	Likelihood 1–5 (5 severe)	Severity 1–5 (5 Severe)	Seriousness = L x S	Existing controls	Action to be taken
Premises. Collection from public houses.					
Drink and driving issues – offered a drink.	4	5	20	Instructions	Individual counselling. Medical check?
Mugging on exit	3	5	15	Instructions – car at door	Personal alarms. Training Review areas for daytime schedules in difficult areas
Slipping on icy surfaces	1	4	4	None	Sensible footware
Drunks	5	2	10	None	Assertive Behaviour training

The general risk assessment logic diagram details a recommended procedure.

APPENDIX 5

General Risk Assessment Logic Diagram

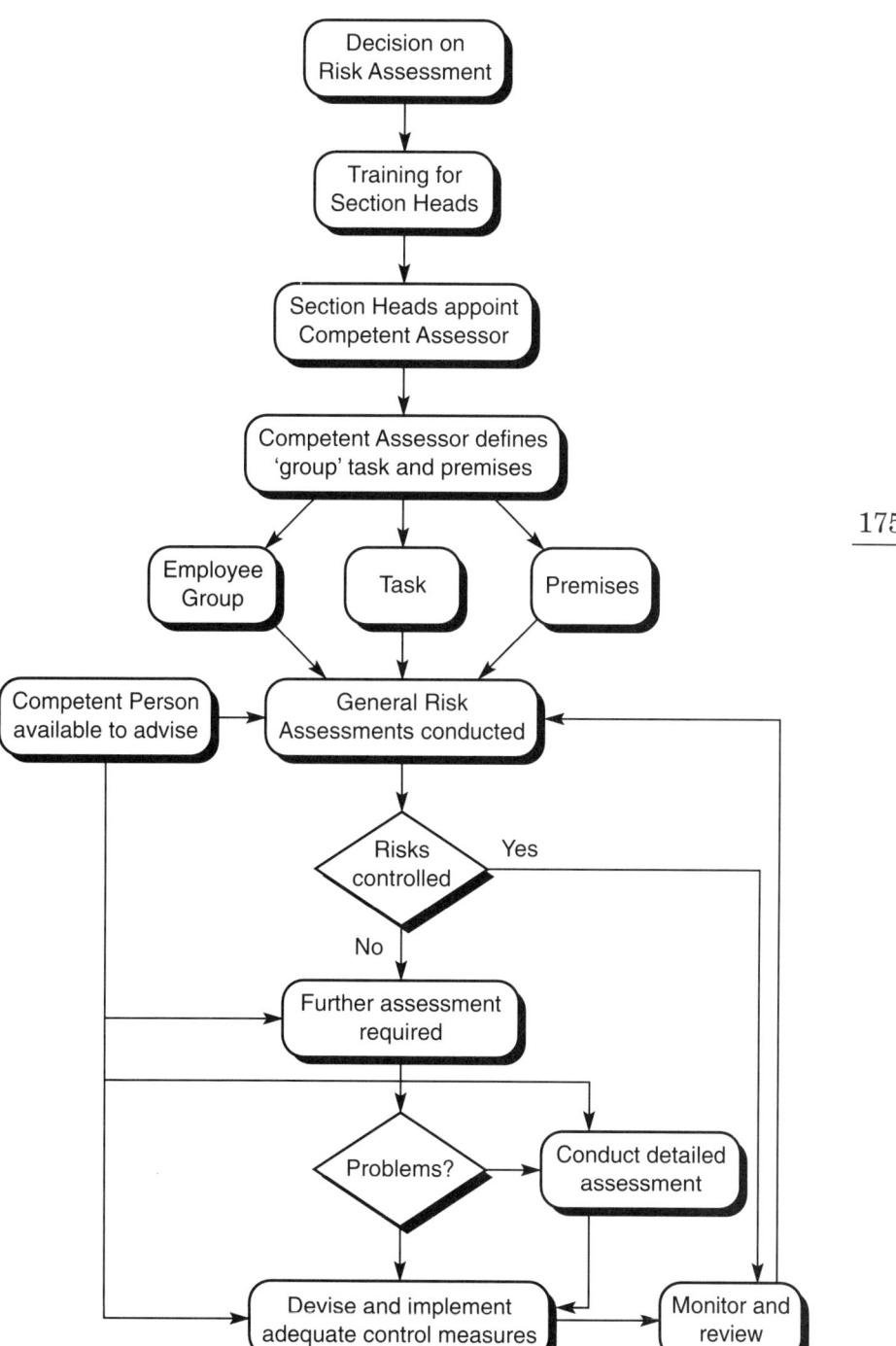

```
Decision on Risk Assessment
        ↓
Training for Section Heads
        ↓
Section Heads appoint Competent Assessor
        ↓
Competent Assessor defines 'group' task and premises
    ↙      ↓      ↘
Employee  Task   Premises
 Group
    ↘      ↓      ↙
Competent Person → General Risk Assessments conducted ←
available to advise                                   │
                     ↓                                │
                Risks controlled ── Yes ──────────────┤
                     │ No                             │
                     ↓                                │
              Further assessment required             │
                     ↓                                │
                  Problems? ──→ Conduct detailed      │
                     ↓              assessment        │
         Devise and implement ←─────┘                 │
         adequate control measures ──→ Monitor and ───┘
                                       review
```

Appendix 6

Safety awareness programme for Lone Workers

■

Session 1: Understanding the dangers of lone working

A discussion session, covering the following points:

- The nature of the task.
- The location, e.g. isolated countryside, industrial estate, residential area. Has the site been visited before?
- Potential risks, e.g. weather conditions, attack by another person, inexperience, night working.

Session 2: Policy? Safe working arrangements

Explanation and discussion to look at:

- Regional lone worker policies.
- Safe working arrangements for lone workers.

Session 3: Management and individual responsibilities

A discussion session to look at:

- Manager's responsibilities, e.g., to assess risks faced by Lone Workers; to provide appropriate control of the work.
- Individual responsibilities, e.g., to take reasonable care of themselves; to co-operate with their employer in the discharge of their legal obligations.

Session 4: Safety equipment

A discussion to look at some of the different types of safety equipment which may be required when lone working, their limitations and correct usage, e.g., personal attack alarms, mobile telephones, emergency packs, etc.

Session 5: Action plans and risk assesment

A discussion session looking at:

- Is there a need for individual and/or departmental action plans for Lone Workers?
- What is risk assessment?
- Why carry out risk assessment?
- How do you carry out risk assessment?

Session 6: Communication skills

A discussion and practical session looking at communication skills in potentially confrontational situations.

- Analysis of 'problem situations', calling on the skills and experience of the group.
- General strategy for handling any situation, e.g., understanding the likely response and attitudes of individuals, considering previous experience, watching for 'signs' that you are not getting across and considering alternative strategies if thought necessary.
- Simple techniques for defusing aggression.

Appendix 7

Useful Addresses

∎

External Victim Support

Victim Support counselling is undertaken by volunteers and is confidential and free to the victim. The National Office is at 39 Brixton Road, London SW9 6DZ. Tel: 071-582 5712.

Health and Safety Executive
Baynards House, 1 Chepstow Place, Westbourne Grove, London W2 4TF Tel: 071-243 6000.

The local police station
The Home Office has a useful leaflet called 'Victims of Crime: how you can help the police to help you', which gives information on how to apply for compensation if employees suffer an injury, loss or damage from crime. The leaflet is available from local police stations.

Management Development Workshops Ltd
Offers workshops designed specifically for Lone Workers and their managers. 4A Collier Lane, Baildon, Shipley, West Yorkshire, BD17 5LN. Tel: 0274 587146.

National Association of Victim Support Schemes
Cranmer House, 39 Brixton Road, London SW9 6DZ. Tel: 071-735 9166.

The Occupational Health Service
The OHS can advise and support victims of violence who are suffering physical, emotional and psychological disturbances following a violent event. Each OHS area will have professional staff who have had specialist training in professional debriefing victims and in counselling skills.

Suzy Lamplugh Trust
14 East Sheen Avenue, London SW14 8AS. Tel: 081-392 1839.

The Tavistock Institute of Human Relations
Offers workshops for managers to help them control violence and abuse to staff who deal directly with the public. Contact the Tavistock Centre, 120 Belsize Lane, London NW3 5BA. Tel: 071-435 7111.

Welfare Department
The Welfare Department can advise and provide useful information on legal issues such as how to claim compensation from the Criminal Injuries Compensation Board. In addition, many of the Welfare Officers have been trained in Victim Support techniques.

Bibliography

A *Guide to the Health and Safety at Work Act, 1974.*
A *Guide to Safe Travel*
The Suzy Lamplugh Trust, London.
Brown, Robert, Bute, Stanley and Ford, Peter, *Social Workers at Risk: The Prevention and Management of Violence*, Macmillan Education Ltd., London (1986).
Bugentall, J.E.T., McGraw-Hill, New York (1967).
Buss, A.H., *The Psychology of Aggression*, Wiley, New York (1961).
Cashco (Royal Mail), *Why Me?*, Occupational Health Service.
Froggatt, Helen and Stamp, Paul, *Managing Pressure at Work*, BBC Books, London (1991).
Health and Safety Executive, *Violence to Staff*, free HSE leaflet based on Poyne, B. and Warne, C. *Violence to Staff: A Basis for Assessment and Prevention,* HSE/HMSO (1986).
James and Jongeward, *Born to Win*, Addison-Wesley, Philippines (1971).
Kirsta, Alix, *The Book of Stress Survival – How to Live Positively*, Unwin Paperbacks, London (1986).
Lamplugh, Diana, *Beating Aggression – A Practical Guide for Working Women*, Weidenfeld and Nicholson, London (1988).
Lamplugh, Diana, *Without Fear – The Key to Staying Safe*, Weidenfeld and Nicholson, London (1991).
Management of Violence, Macmillan Education Ltd., London (1986).
Maslow, A.H., *Self Actualisation and Beyond in Challenges of Humanistic Psychology* (ed.)
Moyer, K.E, *The Psychology of Aggression.*
Norris, D., *Violence against Social Workers – The implications for Practice*, Kingsley, London (1985).
Phillips & Stockdale, *The Risks in Going to Work.*
Poyne, B. and Warne, C., *Preventing Violence to Staff*, Tavistock Institute of Human Relations – HMSO, London.
Reducing the Risk, Suzy Lamplugh Trust, London.
'Safety First – Advice for Women on Personal Safety', published by South Yorkshire Police.
Sheffield City Council Social Services Department, *Guidance and Procedures to Employees to Assist in the Management of Violence by Clients or Members of the Public.*

Siann, Gerde, *Accounting for Aggression – Perspectives on Aggression*, Allen and Unwin, London (1985).

Surrey County Council Social Services Department, *Guidelines When Working with Tension and Violence*, (1987).

'Tackling Violence at Work', IDS Study 458, 1 May 1990.

Thompson, James, *Coping with Disaster – A Guide Book for Helpers and Survivors*, British Psychological Society, London (1989).

Travel Safely by Public Transport, (compiled by the Department of Transport and the Suzy Lamplugh Trust with the co-operation of London Underground Ltd., The Bus and Coach Council, British Rail and the British Transport Police), the Department of Transport (April 1991).

Woods, Mike, *The New Manager*, Element Books, Shaftesbury (1989).

Woods, Mike, *The Aware Manager,* Element Books, Shaftesbury (1989).

Index

ACTH, 129
actions to reduce incidents, 48
aggression
  definitions, 69
  Health and Safety Executive
    definition, 71
  sociological school, 70
Alan, 1
  balance of order and disorder, 25
  hierarchy of needs, 21
  incident recording and analysis, 42
  learning from others, 41
  personal stress strategy, 25
  playing games, 21
  personal maintenance, 67
  setting of personal norms and standards, 20
  stress relief, 24
  time structure, 30
  working with the FRAME, 17
anxiety, process of handling, 137
appropriate assertion
  dealing with criticism, 122
  examples of use, 123
assailants, assumptions and stereotypes, 45
assaults
  British Crime Survey of 1988 figures, 73
  casual, 71
  Debbie incident, 127
  ratio of men to women, 72
  verbal, 71
attacks
  Health Service and Royal Mail, 36
  Labour Research Department statistics, 72
  Suzy Lamplugh Trust data, 72
attitude loop, 107–9
  using the STOP sign, 109
attitudes, non-verbal behaviour as indicator, 105
balance of private life and work, 25, 31
balance of risk, 102
Bandler and Grinder, 94
Barbara, 1

balance of order and disorder, 25
externally imposed discipline, 28
BBC, Publication on stress, 131
belief system
  I MUST, 116
  others, 114
belief systems
  helping, 155
  hierarchy, 113
  overall purpose of universe, 113
  perfectionism, 114
  strength, 114
  superiority, 114
  urgency, 114
  work ethic, 114
British Telecom, pamphlet, 46
broken record, 117
  dealing with criticism, 121
Bruce Lee, 149
case study
  Barber Shop, 40
  bouncy salesman, 100
  brief examples of action to prevent incidents, 48
  building site and safety equipment, 55
  change in practice due to recording and analysis, 42
  changing situations, 78
  computer specialist, 16
  dangerous cliff, 74
  Darren the football supporter, 136
  Debbie and the assault, 127
  delivery of Giros, 47
  DHSS Direct Payments, 38
  dog repellents, 56
  door to door salesman and inherited attitudes, 110
  dress for the occasion, 85
  Eileen and the angry farmer, 58
  hospital receptionist, 90
  ignored alarm, 76
  injury away from support, 37
  lecturer with an 'attitude problem', 105
  mental health nurse assault, 46
  mental nurse in role conflict, 64

mental nurse in changed professional
   objectives, 65
mental nurse promised what he could
   not give, 65
Mr and Mrs Green, 77
newspaper stand and refusal of change, 46
Park Warden under pressure, 117
Patrick and anxiety, 137
prejudice and the Personnel Manager, 135
professional distancing, 125
race attitudes and the STOP sign, 109
racially based preconceptions, 85
riding school and abusive phone calls, 46
salesman with the unexpected
   challenge, 67
sexual discrimination, 150
Social Security office procedural
   changes, 50
Sophie Mirman and Sock Shop, 42
use of relaxation techniques, 139
catastrophe spiral, 108
checklist for working away from the
   worksite
   employees and managers, 53
code of practice, 51
   car passengers, 51
   criteria for development, 51
   cynical comments, 54
   informal safety guidelines, 157
   special problems, 51
   tracing, 50
commitment, importance of 'top down', 57
Common Law
   relation to H&S@WA, 36
   Tort of Negligence, 36
communication, mismatch, 104
constructive enquiry
   explanation, 123
   learning from criticism, 122
consultation
   importance of, 54
   training programmes, 54
contact addresses, 178
core rules, 18
criticism
   dealing with criticism, 119
   giving criticism, 124
   practicalities of giving, 124
   techniques for giving, 125
   triggering negative internal dialogue, 120
Dan, 27
   people 'fix', 30
   scheduling for self discipline, 28

time structure, 30
danger, factors that reduce effect of, 133
Darren, 136
Data Protection Act
   relevance to case files, 45
debates – self defence and equality, 148
Debbie, 127
diagnosis
   incident recording and analysis, 42
   learning from others, 41
   risk assessment, 41
Diana Lamplugh
   Better Safe than Sorry, 35
   discussion of Codes of Practice, 51
   factors in Suzy's disappearance, 58
dress, 85
   freedom to choose as motivator, 18
EC regulations, 36, 172–175
Eileen
   issues of empathy, 94
   meeting the angry farmer, 58
   personal stress, 67
   roles and behaviour, 99
   roles and tactics, 63
Ellis, Albert, 112
empathy, 93
   maintenance, 100
employees, categories at risk, 46
empowerment – loss of, 25
environment of incidents, 47
equality, 150
establishing safe working procedures,
   39–40
   guidelines for safe working, 49
exercises
   controlling pressure, 28
   defining personal FRAMEs, 20
   discrepancy in job objectives, 66
   invading space, 89
   lying is impossible, 106
   objectives – personal and
      organisational, 60
   personally difficult situations, 116
   practising establishing empathy using
      'positions', 97
   professional distancing, 126
   professional objectives, 62
   red, amber, and green situations, 79
role conflict, 62
sincere or insincere, 89
stress map, 25
structuring time, 30
time diary of stress, 26

using appropriate assertion and
  constructive enquiry, 123
using appropriate assertion – words and
  phrases that offend, 88
fielding, 118
  dealing with criticism, 121
fourth position
  role of the producer, 96
  the right messenger?, 99
FRAME, definition, 18
Francis, life plan, 34
Frank, role conflict, 65
Freud, Eros and Thanatos, 25
General Adaptation Syndrome, 130
General Health Questionnaire, 168
George, red, amber and green
  situations, 79
Golding, William, 70
Guardian Newspaper, advertisement
  illustrating preconceptions, 135
guidelines for safe working
  central notification of working site, 49
  culture change, 49
Harry, role conflict to abuse, 65
hazards, intrinsic danger, 73
he who dares wins attitude, 70
Health and Safety at Work Act
  provisions, 36
  safety in laboratories, 78
Health and Safety Regulations, EC
  Directives, 172
health care, monitoring changes, 49
HSE, 179
Ian, fight or run, 67
identification cards, 156
impact of events questionnaire, 167
individual psychological needs, 9
internal dialogue, 107
  Ellis classification, 112
  examples of positive and negative, 111
  positive and negative, 108
jobs
  environment, 8
  ideal fit, 7
  intrinsic danger, 150
  recruitment policy, 151
John, the bouncy salesman, 100
Kevin, 105
  attitudes and non-verbal behaviour, 107
legal responsibilities, issues of Common
  Law and H&S@WA, 36
Lionel, professional distancing, 125

lone worker profile, 3
Management Development Workshops
  Ltd, 179
managing the lone worker, 13
  assisting with recovery from traumatic
    incident, 147
  defining WHATs not HOWs, 19
Martina Navratilova, 49
messages
  basic rules, 82
  professional and secondary, 98
messages, messengers and shadows, 82–83
Metropolitan Police, 151
National Association of Victim Support
  Schemes, 179
negative internal dialogue
  origins, 110
  review to reduce anxiety, 138
  triggered by criticism, 120
non-verbal behaviour
  distance and space, 89
  indicator of attitudes, 106
objectives
  common ground, 60
  professional and motivational
    objectives, 65
Occupational Health Executive, role in
  giving advice, 146
Occupational Health Service, 178
PACE, 101
passive or aggressive attitudes, strategy
  to avoid, 108
passivity, response to negative internal
  dialogue, 110
Patrick, 137
  using the STOP sign, 109
personal factors
  expectation of blame, 43
  feeling of guilt, 43
  messengers and shadows, 81
  reaction to danger, 133
  showing empathy, 93
  unacceptable risk, 75
  values and beliefs, 60
personal maintenance, 67
personal motivation, 10
  jobs and companionship, 10
  self motivation, 20
personal space, risks of invading, 89
physical characteristics, 85
planning for an effective communication, 97
  clarity of purpose, 98

contingencies, 99
maintaining empathy, 100
roles and agenda, 99
tactics, 98
poker faces, 107
positions
  dealing with criticism, 124
  first, second, third and fourth positions, 94
  role of Director, 95
  the fourth position – the producer, 96
  third position – technique, 95
Post Traumatic Stress Disorder
  behaviours related to, 143
  observable symptoms, 143
pre-conceptions, 84
preventative procedures
  problems of ignoring, 76
  understating of risk, 45
professional and secondary messages, 102
professional distancing, 125
prognosis
  case files, 44
  collation and classification of data, 44
  setting up priorities, 44
questionnaire, trait anxiety, 131
receptionist
  case study, 90
  looking at positions, 96
  professional and secondary messages, 98
relationships, job, environment and job holder, 6
relaxation
  breath control, 140
  techniques, 139
reporting procedures
  reasons for unreported incidents, 43
resisting pressure, 117
  broken record, 117
  fielding, 118
  workable compromise, 119
resources to remain in control, 32
risk, 73–74 and 173–175
  concept of personally acceptable risk, 74
  concept of personally unacceptable, 75
risk assessment
  EC directives, 173
  example of Pools collector, 173
  flow chart for implementation, 175
  formalisation, 41
  learning from others, 41
  talking to people who know, 41
  use of surveys and discussions, 41

Robert Burns, 124
role conflict, table relating to Eileen, 62
roles, tactical issues, 63
Rover Group, 151
rules of effective communication, 102
safety equipment, 55–56
  as an aspect of life, 55
  basic rule for lone workers, 55
  car phones, 56
  dog repellents, 56
  personal alarms, 56
safety guidelines, 156
self actualisation
  setting 'little tasks', 21
self defence, 148
Selye, H, 130
shadows
  effect of hostile, 91
  effect on the message, 91
  positive and negative, 84
'sorry', trigger to negative internal dialogue, 121
stages to establish safe working, 40
STOP sign., 109
  use in rethinking anxiety, 138
stress, 23
  alarm reaction, 130
  assessing personal 170
  balance of 'people needs', 27
  burn-out, 24
  debriefing, 144
  distinctions between invigorating and disabling, 23
  events that provide, 128
  fight or run (flight), 67, 129
  individual differences, 130
  lack of personal maintenance, 67
  loss of empowerment, 25
  mechanism, 128
  recalled experience, 142
  rust-out, 24
  trait anxiety, 131
stress counselling, 163
structuring time, five elements, 29
support mechanisms, 27, 33
Suzy Lamplugh Trust
  address, 179
  film, 75
  reasons for, 39
  safety guidelines, 156
  statistics of attacks, 72
Tavistock Institute of Human Relations, 179

time diary, 33
total communication
  issues, 104
  messenger, message and shadow, 90
  summary, 104
  the receptionist, 90
traffic light principle, 77–80
  amber for care, 77
  changing lights, 77
  examples of situations, 79
  green for safety, 76
  red for danger, 76
  use in planning a meeting, 97

training, the need for, 57
training programme, 176
trait anxiety, 131
trauma counselling, 144
traumatic incident
  factor against recovery, 147
  factors helping return to stability, 144, 146
  role of the manager, 147
type A and type B, 24
words and language, 86–87
workable compromise, 119
working needs questionnaire, 11–13